HOME ECONOMICS 2.0

Cooking for two on a budget

Jane Ashley

Most of the recipes are ones we've been cooking in our family for years. They could have originally come from my wide collection of cookbooks and magazines, but have been adapted to fit our lifestyle of healthy budget eating. A lot of the newer recipes are from a mixture of traditional meals from around the world found on the internet and adapted by me.

Raw or semi-cooked eggs should not be consumed by babies, toddlers, pregnant or breastfeeding women, the elderly or those suffering from a chronic illness.

The recipe prices correspond to supermarket prices in October 2018.

Copyright © Jane Ashley 2018

Text © 2018 Jane Ashley
Photography © 2018 PhilAshley.com
Designed by Jane Ashley
Recipe tested by Jane Ashley

10 9 8 7 6 5 4 3 2 1

Printed in Italy

Published in 2018 by Green Daisy, 12 The Close, Isleworth, Middlesex TW7 4BL

A CIP catalogue record for this book is available from the British Library.

ISBN: 978-1-9164971-0-8

HOME ECONOMICS 2.0
Cooking for two on a budget

Jane Ashley

Published by Green Daisy

Contents

WHY I WROTE ANOTHER
cooking on a budget book

When I finished my last cookbook *Home Economics, How to eat like a king on a budget,* I felt that I'd only just started sharing my hints and tips for frugal cooking. I had really struggled with which recipes to put in it and felt that I'd missed out on so many deserving ones. It's a bit like visiting a Cats Home and wanting to take them all home. (If I wasn't married and didn't have Phil stopping me, I would so be that crazy cat lady.)

I was asked a few times by friends and family if the recipes in the last book could be halved, as there were only two of them - either they hadn't started a family or their children had already flown the nest. So I decided to write this book with those people in mind and budgeted it for two with a weekly food menu.

When our daughter went off to university, it was a real challenge to get used to just cooking for two again. We had a lot of wasted food or overate to use it up. It reminded me of before we were parents, with our meals mainly consisting of expensive ready-made dishes you shoved in the oven or a dodgy takeaway.

Of course you can double most of the recipes for four or more, in the same way that my first book's recipes can be halved for two. But this time I've worked them out to save the most money and use as many of the ingredients as possible when cooking for two, without resorting to just rice every day. I've also only used free-range chickens and eggs, so the budgets are a little higher, by £3 a chicken, but that's your choice. When there are leftover ingredients I try to give suggestions of lunches and treats that can be made to use them up and save on food waste. Sometimes I've brought larger amounts of dried goods, like rice and flour, as it makes economic sense, and they will last. It is more expensive to cook for two instead of four per serving, but that doesn't mean you need to compromise on quality and taste. Some of the following dishes can be made for as little as 60p each.

As well as lots of delicious budget recipes, I've included a few simple step-by-step pages to help you to save even more, plus a few lunch ideas to save you picking up a takeaway sandwich on your way to work. Did you know that if a couple bring in their own lunch every day they could save over £2,000 a year? Just think what you could do with all that money!

Like you, I'm not a chef, I can't do that fancy chopping thing, so it takes me a bit longer in the kitchen. I do like to have everything prepared as much as possible before I start so I'm not hunting around for mixed spice while the pan boils over. If you read my other book you'll know that I came to cooking quite late. I'd already left home for a few years before I learnt to cook proper meals. So nothing in this book should be too challenging or need anything but the most basic equipment. I did try to work a blowtorch in to my recipes, but Phil talked me into seeing reason. Anyway I hope you enjoy trying these recipes, and save yourself plenty of money.

TOP TIPS
To save you money

1   Always shop with a list. Preferably in some kind of order – fruit and veg together, dairy together, etc.

2   Do a proper inventory of what you need to buy. Make a list of meals for the week and stick to it. We keep a mini notice board on the fridge door and jot down when something from the store cupboard runs out. This can then quickly be added to the weekly shopping list.

3   Delivered meal boxes might seem like a great idea, and they're probably a good stepping stone if you're not used to shopping and cooking from scratch. However, they can work out to be quite expensive, when you can just find the recipes you want and order the ingredients you need online. Save some money and just do it yourself.

4   Never go shopping when you are hungry or hungover, you'll end up filling the trolly with cakes and biscuits.

5   Try to check item prices, as supermarkets always seem to be putting prices up or down. If it's expensive that week, swap in something similar, be a bit flexible. They also sometimes have one product priced by the gram next to a similar product priced by the kilogram or even per item. I'm sure it's to confuse you.

6   Always try to buy the supermarket's cheaper own brand products. There really isn't much difference in flavour. Why pay 3 times as much for the same raw ingredients?

7   Don't get too hung up on the dates. The only date you really need to worry about on food labelling is the use-by date. The sell-by date is for the shop's own turn around, the best before date is when it's at its optimum freshness. Take a sniff first if you're not sure, just don't mess around with meat or fish. Put them in the freezer to last longer, and cook on the same day you defrost.

8   I try to buy seasonal vegetables when they're cheaper, and use them to make soups to freeze. But buying frozen vegetables is another way to save money. You only need to take out what you're using, so there won't be food waste. Frozen vegetables will also have a higher nutritional value as they'll have been frozen close to picking.

9   Batch cook if you have space. Put aside one day a month to cook lots of delicious meals ready for the coming weeks. You're less likely resort to a takeaway after a busy day if you have a tasty homemade meal in the fridge or freezer waiting for you.

10. I don't tend to bother with the food with discounted yellow stickers, as if you've written out a meal plan you'll end up saving a lot more than the odds and ends with those deals. Of course if it's something you usually buy and it can be frozen, go for it. The same applies to bread and milk. We tend to put one in the fridge and one in the freezer to save it going out of date before it's used.

STOCK CUPBOARD ESSENTIALS

I don't know about you, but when I was growing up, my family didn't really use many herbs or spices in our cooking. There was a wooden spice rack sitting on the wall that was slightly dusty, with the usual dried leaves all a sort of pale green colour. Dried rosemary, dried parsley, dried thyme – like a Simon and Garfunkel song but dried.

In the 80s exotic food had yet to be mainstream like it is today. A takeaway curry didn't have the complexity of flavours that we are used to now. It was just hot and pretty tasteless. And Thai food, forget that, we didn't know where that was, let alone eat the food.

When you first start to cook curries and international dishes, there seems like an endless number of spices to use, but really there are just a few that are used in most of them. Listed below are the most commonly used ones so there's really is no need to buy too many in one go.

If budgets allow, it is more cost effective to buy larger bags of spices from the world food aisle instead of the little pots you'll see in the herb section. You could always go halves with a friend to spread the cost and decant them into your own clean jam jars, just don't forget to label them!

This also applies to vinegars and oils. A good quality extra virgin olive oil is great for salad dressings, but you can use just a plain olive oil if you have to. There are lots of fancy oils out there, but I mostly just use those and a vegetable oil. Rapeseed is recomended as the best oil for general frying, and most UK vegatable oil tends to be rapeseed, just check the label.

Vinegars again can be a minefield. Apart from normal malt (chip) vinegar, the other one I can't do without is balsamic. This can range in price from £1 to over £50. Depending on whether it's original or balsamic de Modena is an inexpensive imitation that I think is fine for most cooking. If you also get inexpensive white wine and red wine vinegars you've got your bases covered for most dishes.

Below is an essential list of everyday stock cupboard ingredients you'll need to make all the meal recipes in this cookbook. All of the items are usual ingredients most people would have in their larder – there should be nothing scary, expensive or difficult to find.

From the larder:
Pepper
Salt
Sugar
Tabasco
English mustard
Dijon mustard
Wholegrain mustard
Black mustard seeds
Olive oil
Stock cubes
Cloves
Ground ginger
Ground nutmeg
Mixed herbs
Ground allspice

Cayenne pepper
Ground cumin
Cumin seeds
Coriander seeds
Ground coriander
Paprika
Peppercorns
Chilli flakes
Turmeric
Chilli powder
Garam masala
Runny honey
Cider vinegar
Red wine vinegar
White wine vinegar
Balsamic vinegar

Cinnamon
Dried oregano
Dried thyme
Baking powder or bicarb
Rapeseed oil
Olive oil
Extra virgin olive oil
Gherkins
Capers
Fish sauce
Quick yeast
Yeast flakes (vegan)
Mayonnaise
Ketchup
Worcestershire sauce
Soy sauce

Tomato purée
Dry polenta
Mint sauce
Xanthan gum (gluten-free)
Cornflour
Flaked almonds
Sultanas
Cashews

Fresh from the garden:
Sage leaves
Rosemary
Mint
Bay leaves
(If you don't have any fresh, just use dried.)

WHAT TO DO WITH LEFTOVERS

The average household throws away so much food, it's quite criminal when there are people going without in some families. So as well as not buying too much, we also need to try to waste as little as possible. Slightly stale bread and the crusts that no one seems to like should go in the freezer to be made into bread crumbs for a later recipe.

Most of our bread and rolls will go in the freezer to extend their shelf life too, but make sure to cover them completely or they'll get freezer burns and frost damage.

Milk is another great ingredient to freeze, which will save the run out to the shops in your slippers to get a pint for your morning cup of tea.

In our house, chicken normally gets jointed and put in freezer bags if we're not eating it straight away. I even save the carcasses until I have 3 or 4 to boil down with an onion, carrot and celery for fresh stock, which in turn gets frozen until needed. I only have a standard size freezer, but as its not full of ready meals, I make the most of its space to save on food waste. Remember the golden rule though, you can't re-heat chicken more than once after it's cooked.

As well as not over-buying ingredients every time you go shopping, you can save time and money by interlocking meals in the week. For example, cooking a Bolognese sauce and using half of it for enchiladas or making pasta and saving some back for a cold pasta salad for lunch the next day can all add up over the year to save you more money.

Most meals can be chilled for a few days in the fridge, just make sure they're completely cooled and covered properly. You don't want to get sick because of cross contamination. For example, raw meats and fish should be covered and kept at the bottom of the fridge so as not to accidently spill any blood on to other food items. Cooked ingredients should be on a higher shelf and again covered in case of spillage from other ingredients.

I tend to keep my vegetables and salad ingredients in separate draws, but if you only have one, try to keep them at separate ends. This will save for example on tomatoes getting squashed by heavy potatoes.

I used to put fresh herbs on the window sill in water. But talking to a home economist I found out they'll last longer with a spritz of water and in an airtight plastic bag in the fridge.

Ever opened a bag of salad and found one side all mushy and black. That seems to happen if it's in contact with the side of the fridge where it'll get too cold. Always try to keep salad and leafy herbs away from the edges. That goes for soft fruits, like strawberries too. Keep an eye on the fridge temperature as well.

A great way to save money and power is to batch cook. Set aside a weekend once a month if you can to make up a few meals to put in the fridge or freezer for those busy days. That way you won't be tempted to order a takeaway when you get in late. Just make sure you label them correctly or you could end up with Bolognese on your rice instead of chilli.

I also sometimes make up bags of cooked onions, carrots, and celery, then freeze them for sauces, risottos and stews. It saves on food waste and time preparing mid-week meals.

Let the freezer help out as much as possible, but just make sure you keep an eye on dates and when you put items in. We all have that unidentified tupperware box of stew or chilli lurking at the back somewhere that you can't remember even cooking.

HOW TO MAKE
garlic naan & peshwari naan

You know how when you go out for a curry the naans and chapatis are so delicious, but when you try to do your own curry night at home it's never the same from the supermarket. Well, with this recipe you'll need never be disappointed again. I've given you 2 recipes for the most popular naans that'll take your homemade curries up to the next level.

Makes 6 naans

Ingredients for the naan dough:
1 teaspoon quick yeast
1 teaspoon caster sugar
1/2 teaspoon salt
300g strong flour, plus extra for rolling
1 tablespoon olive oil
150ml natural yogurt

Ingredients for the peshwari paste:
1 1/2 tablespoons of desiccated coconut
1 teaspoon caster sugar
50g flaked almonds
10 sultanas
2 tablespoons single cream, or coconut cream

Ingredients for the garlic butter:
1 tablespoon butter, melted
1 tablespoon olive oil
1 garlic clove, crushed
Few sprigs of finely chopped coriander

To make the dough, in a large bowl mix the dry ingredients together, and form a well in the middle. Pour in the oil and yogurt. Gather in the sides with your hands and mix together well.

Knead for 10 minutes, then cover the bowl with cling film and put in a warm place for an hour to prove and rise. I use my oven set at 40°C

While the dough is proving, you can make the peshwari paste. Whizz all the dry ingredients together in a blender or with a hand blender, then add the cream to form a solid paste. Set aside.

When the naan dough has risen, divide into 6 balls, then flatten slightly with your hand. Pop a 2cm piece of peshwari paste in the centre of each one, then fold up the sides to cover it.

On a floured surface roll out each ball in a teardrop shape to about 25cm long, with the peshwari filling trapped inside.

Stack the naans up with a light dusting of flour between, to stop them sticking together.

Heat up a dry non-stick frying pan. Brush off the flour and toast the bread on each side for a couple of minutes, until golden and puffed up.

Brush both sides of the naan with plain melted butter, or garlic butter if not using the paste. Keep warm in a low oven until ready to serve.

To make the garlic butter, melt the butter for 10 seconds in a microwave, and mix with all the other ingredients.

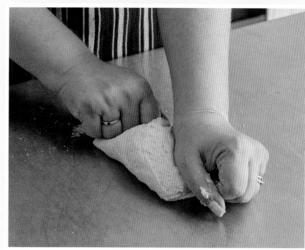

GARLIC DOUGH BALLS
& fried pizza bread

Not long ago we went on a road trip around Italy with my parents for a little holiday. We ended up near one of the lakes where we tried these tasty fried pizza bread bites. I arranged it so we ended up going back to the same restaurant the next night just so I could order them again. They're that delicious, and no one minded as it was a lovely place overlooking Lake Como.

Serves 2

Ingredients for the dough balls:
250g strong white bread flour
$1/2$ teaspoon salt
$1/2$ teaspoon sugar
$1/2$ tablespoon oil
$1/2$ teaspoon quick yeast
150ml warm water

Ingredients for the garlic butter:
1 tablespoon butter, softened
1 tablespoon oil
2 garlic cloves
Handful of parsley

Ingredients for the pizza dough:
250g strong white bread flour
$1/2$ teaspoon salt
$1/2$ teaspoon sugar
$1/2$ tablespoon oil
$1/2$ teaspoon quick yeast
150ml warm water
Vegetable oil, for frying
Handful of chopped parsley

For the dough balls, place the flour and salt into a large bowl, stir in the sugar and yeast, then rub in the oil. Add enough water to form a soft sticky dough. Knead the dough on a floured surface for about 10 minutes, until smooth.

Divide the dough into 6 or 8 small pieces and roll them into balls, then place on an oiled baking tray with space around them. Cover with cling film and leave in a warm place for 20 minutes, or until they have doubled in size.

Preheat the oven to 220°C.

Bake the dough balls for 10 minutes, then reduce the temperature to 200°C and cook for a further 6-8 minutes, or until golden brown.

Make the garlic butter while this is cooking by chopping the garlic finely with the parsley and adding to the oil and softened butter.

Serve the dough balls in a bowl with the butter mixture brushed over them.

For the pizza dough, start the same way as the dough balls, but instead of making 6 to 8 small balls leave as one, then pop it in a bowl with cling film over the top and set aside in a warm place. Ideally 30-40°C for about 30 minutes.

Once the dough has risen it is ready to be rolled out and divided in two. On a flour-dusted surface, roll out each until roughly 30cm in diameter and 5mm thick.

Heat a small frying pan over a high heat, add about 1cm of vegetable oil and carefully fry the pizza dough for about 1 minute on each side. Remove with tongs and drain on kitchen paper. Cut into slices and scatter with chopped parsley.

HOW TO MAKE FRESH PASTA
farfalle or bow ties

There's nothing as nice as fresh pasta, but it can be quite expensive to buy in the supermarket. I've not even seen gluten-free or vegan versions, So I thought I'd show you how quick and easy it is to rustle up a batch, whatever your dietary needs.

Serves 2 with leftovers

Ingredients for the fresh pasta:
200g plain flour, plus extra for rolling
$1/2$ tablespoon salt
75ml water
1 egg

Ingredients for the fresh vegan pasta:
200g plain flour
$1/2$ tablespoon salt
85ml water

Ingredients for the gluten-free pasta:
150g gluten free bread flour, plus extra for rolling
1 teaspoon Xanthan gum
$1/2$ tablespoon salt
70ml water
$1/2$ tablespoon oil
1 egg

Using '00' flour:
Traditionally you would use Italian '00' flour, but I normally make mine with just plain flour, and if you're on a budget you don't really want to go buying expensive different flours.

Simple pasta salad recipe:
2 teaspoons finely chopped red onion
1 teaspoon capers
1 tablespoon pesto
2 teaspoons olive oil
185g tin tuna in spring water, drained
100g leftover pasta shapes
3 sun-dried tomatoes, chopped

You can make this on a large, clean, flat work surface or in a bowl if you prefer. Firstly, make a well in the centre of your dry ingredients to contain the wet ingredients.

Pull in the sides and mix together well then knead on a floured surface for about 5-10 minutes, until it goes springy. Add more flour or water if you need to.

Put the dough in cling film and leave in the fridge for at least 1 hour.

If you don't have a pasta machine, a tip I learned in a cookery class was to start at one end and roll a section of the dough, then let that hang over the edge of your work surface while you roll out more, until you have rolled it all section by section. Make sure not to let it touch the floor.

Once rolled out, slice thinly in to 3cm strips, then cut these every 7cm with a decorative cutter if you have one.

Pinch the middle of each piece together with your fingers, adding a drop of water to help it stick.. Then sprinkle with flour and leave to harden for at least 30 minutes to hold their shape.

Now put the water on to boil, making sure you use your largest pan so the pasta has room to move. When the water is boiling, add the pasta and simmer for about 3-4 minutes, until just soft (6-8 minutes for gluten-free).

Once it's cooked, drain in a large colander. You can stir in a tablespoon of olive oil or pesto to stop it sticking together.

Serve hot with your favourite sauce or leave to cool and make the simple pasta salad.

HOW TO COOK
perfect rice and rice salad

I know some people are scared of cooking rice – they may have had a bad experience, and I know from my own learning-to-cook days, how hard it is to get burnt rice off the bottom of a pan. But that's no excuse for buying those expensive microwave pouches. They can be more than three times the price of buying normal rice.

Makes 4 servings

Ingredients for the rice salad:
1 cup or 180g rice
(long grain, brown, basmati or wild rice)
400g tin mixed beans, drained and rinsed
162g (1/2 tin) sweetcorn, drained
1 small red onion, finely sliced
1 red pepper, diced
zest and juice of 1 lime
1 teaspoon honey
1 teaspoon white wine vinegar
1 teaspoon olive oil
1 red chilli, finely sliced
Small bunch of coriander, chopped
Pinch of salt and pepper

Added options ingredients:
Chopped up roasted vegetables work well too

Safety tips:
When leaving rice to cool down for salads, chill it as soon as you can by running it under cold water. Drain and either make the salad straight away, or refrigerate until needed. No more than a day or 2.

If you're reheating the rice, make sure it's steaming hot. Do not reheat more than once.

To cook basmati rice follow the instructions below.

Firstly, measure out the rice and put in a saucepan.

Wash the rice with cold water. Swish around and drain, then repeat the process twice more. Now measure out 2 cups of cold water and add to the rice, with 1/2 teaspoon of salt.

Bring to the boil, uncovered and stir once. Then turn down the heat and simmer on low covered with a lid.

Simmer the rice for 5-7minutes. Do not take the lid off until the time is up, as the rice is steam-cooked as much as boiled.

You'll know when it's done as when you take a peek after 5 minutes or so the surface of the rice will have dimples. A clear saucepan lid is ideal for this.

You'll need twice as much water for brown and wild rice and these will need draining after cooking too. Brown rice needs 30-35 minutes simmering and wild rice needs 45-50 minutes, until the kernels start to pop.

When the rice is done, fluff it with a fork and serve hot, or cold for a rice salad.

For the salad, rinse the cooked rice under cold water to cool down and to stop it continuing to cook.

Mix it in a bowl with the beans, sweetcorn, onion and red peppers. In another bowl mix together the lime, vinegar, oil, honey and chilli.

Pour it over the rice mixture, and stir well, then season with a pinch of salt and pepper to taste and mix through the chopped coriander before serving.

HOW TO MAKE
meatballs & burgers

After the scandal of horsemeat found in some supermarket ready meals a few years ago, I think it's more important than ever to make as much of your food from real ingredients as you can. Take burgers for example. Some ready-made ones don't contain 100% beef! But if they don't, what else do they contain? You know that if you buy 100% plain mince from the supermarket that's what you're going to get.

Serves 2

Ingredients for simple burger patties:
250g beef mince
Pinch of salt and pepper
Rapeseed oil, for frying

Ingredients for mozzarella meatballs:
250g beef mince
50g mozzarella, cubed
Pinch of salt and pepper
Rapeseed oil, for frying

Ingredients for vegan burgers:
200g (¹/₂ tin) chickpeas, drained
170g (¹/₂ tin) sweetcorn, drained
¹/₂ teaspoon paprika
¹/₂ teaspoon ground coriander
¹/₂ teaspoon ground cumin
Zest of ¹/₂ lemon
2 heaped tablespoons plain flour, plus extra for dusting
Pinch of sea salt
Rapeseed oil, for frying

Making your own meatballs and beefburgers is one of the simplest money saving recipes you can do. It's just minced beef with a bit of salt and pepper, mixed together and squashed into patties or rolled into balls. After being popped into the fridge for 30 minutes, they're ready to use. How simple is that?

Of course you can make alternatives to this by adding bread crumbs, cooked onions and an egg to bulk them out.

Try mixing or rolling in different herbs and spices to make Moroccan meatballs for pitta bread, or Cajun seasoned burgers for a spicy hot flavour. Or you can really go to town and make mozzarella filled meatballs to add to your spaghetti sauce.

You also don't have to use beef, you could use minced lamb, pork, chicken or turkey. Whatever you use, you'll know actually what's going in to them and save a bit of money too.

To make the simple burger patties or meatballs, add all the ingredients together, squash together well and shape as shown.

To make the mozzarella meatballs, make a small disc of mince and in the middle place a cube of cheese, then fold each edge up to meet and cover the mozzarella completely.

Fry as you would have the supermarket made burgers or meatballs.

To make the vegan burgers, whizz all the ingredients together in a bowl then shape into patties, They may need a little more oil for cooking.

HOW TO MAKE DIPS

These dips make a healthy, tasty alternative to your usual lunch, and can be kept in the fridge for a few days in a clean jam jar. Serve them with warm pitta bread or make yourself some crudité by cutting celery, cucumber, peppers and carrots into batons. You can even make some pitta chips, by baking the sliced pitta bread in a medium hot oven for 10 minutes until crisp.

Blue cheese dip

150g crème fraîche
50g mayonnaise
75g blue cheese
1 dessertspoon white wine vinegar
1 teaspoon Worcestershire sauce

Mix all the ingredients together and serve with warm pitta bread or cut vegetables

Guacamole

2 avocados, mashed
1 large tomato, deseeded and finely diced
Juice of $1/2$ a lime
Small handful of coriander, chopped
$1/4$ red onion, finely diced
$1/2$ red chilli, finely sliced
Salt and pepper, to taste

Mix all the ingredients together and season to taste. Serve with pitta bread, nachos or on chilli con carne.

Baba ghanoush

1 large aubergine
2 tablespoons olive oil
1 garlic clove, crushed
Juice of $1/2$ a lemon
Small handful of parsley

When you have the oven on, oil and roast the aubergine at 200°C for about 50 minutes until soft and slightly charred

Set aside to cool, then cut in half and scoop out the flesh. Put this in a bowl with the other ingredients and mix together with a fork.

Tomato salsa

3 ripe tomatoes, deseeded and finely diced
Handful of fresh coriander, chopped
$1/4$ red onion, finely diced
1 fresh chilli, finely diced
Juice of 1 lime
1 tablespoon virgin olive oil
Pinch of salt and pepper

Finely chop all the ingredients, then squeeze in the juice of the lime and add 2 tablespoons of oil with a pinch of salt and pepper.

Mix together well and taste to see if it needs more seasoning. Let it rest for a while to marinade.

NEW YORK STYLE SANDWICH

Serves 2

1 small baguette, sliced sideways
Butter, to spread
2 medium tomatoes, thinly sliced
Handful of rocket
Few rings of red onion, finely sliced
8 thin slices of salami
4 thin slices of ham
2 slices of cheese
2 pickled gherkins, thinly sliced
1 teaspoon yellow American mustard
2 teaspoons mayonnaise

Cut the baguette sideways, but not all the way through and spread it out on a chopping board.

Butter each side, then spread the mayonnaise over one side and the mustard over the other.

Now layer up on the mayonnaise side the lettuce, tomato, onion, salami, ham and sliced cheese.

Lastly, add the pickled gherkins and close the sandwich.

Use a cocktail stick to hold each sandwich in place if you need to. Cut in half and share.

With sandwiches this good, why would you bother buying a limp sandwich from a supermarket, or an expensive one from a deli? Making your own lunch can save you over a thousand pounds a year each.

CHRISTMAS SANDWICH

Serves 2

4 slices of white or brown bread
Butter, to spread
A few slices of cooked turkey
2 tablespoons stuffing
2 sausages wrapped in bacon, sliced
2 medium tomatoes , thinly sliced
A few slices of cucumber
Handful of lettuce leaves
2 teaspoons mayonnaise
1 teaspoon cranberry sauce

Alternative vegetarian version:
Substitute the turkey and sausage for Brie cheese

Butter each slice of bread and spread mayonnaise over one slice and cranberry over the other, then add a spread of the stuffing to the cranberry slice.

On the mayonnaise slice layer up the lettuce, tomato and cucumber,

Next add the turkey, and sliced sausage.

Place on the top layer of bread and secure with a cocktail stick.

Serve with picked gherkins and onions.

AUBERGINE & MOZZARELLA SUB

Serves 2

1 small baguette, sliced sideways
30g (¹/₄ packet) of mozzarella, torn
1 small aubergine, sliced
1 teaspoon olive oil
400g (¹/₂ tin) tomatoes
¹/₂ onion, finely sliced
Pinch of fresh Italian or mixed dried herbs
Pinch of salt and pepper
1 garlic clove, finely chopped
1 teaspoon tomato purée
Splash of Worcestershire sauce

Alternative meatball version:
Substitute the aubergine for
6-8 cooked small meatballs (see page 22)

Firstly brush the sliced aubergine with oil and griddle until soft. Or if you're using meatballs for this recipe, (see page 22)

In a saucepan fry the onion and garlic in the olive oil until soft. Then tip in the tomatoes, Worcestershire sauce, tomato purée, herbs, salt and pepper and bring to the boil.

Turn down and simmer for about 20 minutes until reduced and thickened. If using cooked meatballs, add them now to warm through.

Slice open the baguettes and layer in the warm tomato sauce. Next add the aubergine or meatballs, then tear over the mozzarella and microwave for 30 seconds to melt. Cut in half to share.

This can be heated up and assembled at work. I've done it before to the jealous looks of my work colleagues.

BLT & CLUB SANDWICHES

Serves 2

6 slices of bread
4 teaspoons mayonnaise
Handful of lettuce leaves
1 large beef tomato, finely sliced
8 slices of cooked bacon

Alternative club version:
½ chicken breast or equivalent in leftover
chicken for the club sandwich

First slice the chicken and tomato.

Then toast the bread and spread the mayonnaise over each slice.

Take the first slice, mayonnaise side up, and lay on the lettuce and tomato to cover the toast. Now lay on top 2 slices of bacon on each sandwich.

Now lay down the second slice of toast, mayonnaise side up, and put on it another layer of lettuce, tomato, 2 slices of bacon, and if making the club the sliced chicken.

Lastly, pop on the final slice of toast, mayonnaise side down.

Slice in half and use a cocktail stick to hold each sandwich in place. Serve with a few crisps or pickles if you want.

CROQUE MONSIEUR
an amazing toasted cheese sandwich

This is an amazing sandwich that isn't practical to take to work. It's more of a weekend brunch thing for when you get up late, hungover or not. Be warned, this sandwich isn't for the health conscious, but is a great little weekend treat every now and then to set you up for the day.

Serves 2

Ingredients for the white sauce:
125ml milk
125ml cream
20g butter
20g plain flour
1 teaspoon Dijon mustard
1/4 teaspoon nutmeg
Pinch of salt and pepper

4 slices of bread
20g butter
1 teaspoon Dijon mustard
100g grated cheese
4 thin slices of smoked ham

Preheat the oven to 200°C

Next make the white sauce, by melting the butter in a saucepan, then adding the flour and cooking over a low heat for a couple of minutes.

Add the milk and cream and whisk while bringing to a gentle boil. Then add the Dijon mustard, nutmeg and a little salt and pepper. The constancy should be a thick creamy sauce. Allow to cool slightly.

Now toast the bread lightly, and butter.

Spread one side with the Dijon mustard, then a layer of the white sauce.

Next cover the sauce with half the grated cheese, and a slice of the ham.

Then place on top the other slice of bread and spread a layer of the sauce over the top, along with the rest of the grated cheese.

Put the sandwiches in the oven and bake for about 10 minutes, or until the cheese is golden.

Slice in half before serving.

If you want to turn this in to a Croque madame add a fried or poached egg on top.

CURRY PASTA SALAD

Serves 2

150g penne or any pasta
2 tablespoons mayonnaise
2 teaspoons curry paste
40g natural yogurt
Squeeze of lemon juice
2 tablespoons mango chutney
Handful of flaked almonds
Handful of coriander, chopped
6cm cucumber, deseeded and sliced thinly
2 celery sticks, sliced thinly
A few slices of chilli, finely chopped

If you fancy something different from a sandwich for lunch, how about these delicious pasta salads? Simple to make, they're guaranteed to keep you full all afternoon.

Cook the pasta as per the packet instructions, then drain and run under a cold tap to cool quickly. Or use leftover cold pasta from the fridge.

Mix the mayonnaise, yogurt, curry paste and mango chutney together with a squeeze of lemon.

Next, chop the vegetables and add these to the sauce. Give it a good stir before adding the cold pasta.

Stir in the coriander and scatter the almonds and chilli and serve.

BACON & AVOCADO PASTA SALAD

Serves 2

150g penne or any pasta
1 tablespoon sunflower oil
80g streaky bacon, chopped
70g cherry tomatoes, halved
1 large tablespoon pesto
1 avocado, sliced
Handful of rocket leaves
Parmesan and pepper, to serve

Cook the pasta as per the packet instructions, then drain and run under a cold tap to cool quickly. Or use leftover cold pasta from the fridge.

Next, in a frying pan heat the oil and fry the bacon for a few minutes until crispy, then set it to one side.

In a bowl, mix the pasta and pesto then add the chopped tomatoes and stir.

Serve with the bacon, rocket, avocado and Parmesan scattered on top. Add a grind of black pepper to taste.

FRENCH ONION SOUP

Makes 4 servings

Ingredients for the soup:
500g onion, halved and thinly sliced
25g butter
Splash of olive oil
$1/2$ teaspoon sugar
3 garlic cloves, sliced
1 tablespoon plain flour
125ml white wine (optional)
650ml hot vegetable stock

Ingredients for the toast:
4 slices of bread, toasted
70g cheese, grated

Firstly, melt the butter on a medium heat, in a large pan with the oil, then add the onions and fry for about 10 minutes, until slightly softened.

Stir in the sugar and carry on cooking for 15 minutes, until starting to caramelise, constantly stirring so it doesn't burn. The onions will start to turn golden.

Add the garlic to the onions and cook a few minutes more, then add in the flour and cook for a minute more, stirring well, before increasing the heat and adding the wine and the hot vegetable stock giving it all a good mix.

Cover and simmer for 15 minutes. Season to taste.

Serve the soup with toasted bread with grilled cheese on top.

SWEET POTATO SOUP

Makes 4 servings

1 carrot, peeled and roughly chopped
1 celery, stalk roughly chopped
1 medium onion, peeled and roughly chopped
2 garlic cloves, sliced
1 large sweet potato, peeled and sliced
Small bunch of fresh parsley, chopped
2 tablespoons olive oil
1 teaspoon curry powder
1 teaspoon paprika
Salt and freshly ground pepper
1 fresh chilli (optional)
1 stock cube

Heat up a large saucepan with 2 tablespoons of olive oil and add all your chopped and sliced ingredients with the chopped stalks of parsley, the paprika and curry powder, then mix together.

Cook for around 15 minutes, until the carrots have softened and the onion is lightly golden.

Meanwhile boil the kettle and add 750ml of hot water to a stock cube. Add the hot stock and give the soup a good stir, then bring to a boil.

Reduce the heat and simmer for 10 minutes, until the sweet potato is cooked through. Season with salt and pepper.

With a hand blender or liquidizer, pulse the soup until smooth. Scatter on the top a little chopped chilli and parsley.

BUTTERNUT SQUASH SOUP

Makes 4 servings

1 onion, peeled and finely diced
$1/2$ teaspoon red chilli flakes (optional)
1 vegetable stock cube
2 tablespoons olive oil
1 butternut squash, peeled
2 carrots, peeled and finely diced
400g (1 tin) of chickpeas, drained
Salt and pepper
2 sage leaves (optional)

Finely dice the carrots and onion and add to the oil in a large pan.

Soften for about 10 minutes.

While this is cooking, grate the flesh of the butternut squash. Crumble in the vegetable stock cube to the onion mixture and add the squash and 750ml of boiling water.

Next add the chickpeas and chilli if using, then let this simmer for about 15 minutes.

Blitz the soup and season with salt and pepper.

Fry a few sage leaves and slice finely to sprinkle on top if you want.

CREAM OF MUSHROOM SOUP

Makes 4 servings

600g mushrooms, finely chopped
100g butter
2 medium onions, chopped
2 garlic cloves, crushed
2 tablespoons plain flour
1 litre hot vegetable stock
2 bay leaves
4 tablespoons cream
Pinch of salt and pepper, to taste

Heat the butter in a large saucepan and cook the garlic and onions until soft but not browned.

Add the mushrooms, then cook on high heat for 3 minutes. Next, add the bay leaves and flour over the mushrooms, and stir well.

Pour in hot stock, and bring to boil, then simmer for about 10 minutes.

Remove the bay leaves, leave to cool slightly, then blend.

Season to taste with the salt and pepper.

Serve with a tablespoon of cream per bowl and extra pepper.

WEEK 1

1	2 loaves of sliced wholemeal bread	**11**	Fresh ginger
2	Olive spread	**12**	Fresh parsley
3	Salted butter	**13**	Chillies
4	2 pints of milk	**14**	Garlic
5	6 free-range eggs	**15**	1 lemon
6	700g pork ribs	**16**	2.5kg potatoes
7	227g tin pineapple	**17**	500g new potatoes
8	300g bacon	**18**	400g braising steak
9	1kg onions	**19**	4 carrots
10	Fresh coriander	**20**	Celery

21	500ml strong ale	**31**	1.5kg plain flour
22	300g mushrooms	**32**	250g Cheddar cheese
23	500g puff pastry	**33**	Little gem lettuce
24	1kg frozen peas	**34**	Packet of 3 peppers
25	Bunch of spring onions	**35**	Packet of 6 tomatoes
26	1 whole free-range chicken	**36**	1 cucumber
27	1kg rice		
28	1 x 400g tin black beans		
29	500g pasta		
20	1 x 400g tin tomatoes		Shopping list for lunch and dinner for 2 for 7 days

DAY-BY-DAY
MENU FOR WEEK 1

Most people think that if you're trying to save money on your weekly food bill you have to cut out meat, and this can put a lot of people off even trying. So I've come up with a week of budget recipes that contain meat every day. It's all about using the right cuts and making sure you use all of it. In this book I've used free-range chicken and eggs, which are a bit more expensive, as I believe in those welfare stardards. You can save more by using barn raised chicken if you choose.

This week a packet of stewing steak is slow cooked and used in 3 different meals, padded out with vegetables and pasta. The chicken also makes 3 delicious meals including a couple of fancy chicken kievs. Week one of recipes come from all over the world, from Britain to Italy on to the Caribbean and beyond, so there should be plenty in it to keep you interested.

Day 1
Lunch
Cheese on toast

Dinner
BBQ ribs with German potato salad

Day 2
Lunch
Leftover potatoes and salad

Dinner
Slow-cooked beef & ale pie with mash and peas

Day 3
Lunch
BLT sandwich

Dinner
Jerk chicken with rice & black eyed beans

Day 4
Lunch
Cheese salad sandwich

Dinner
Beef ragù pasta bake with salad

Day 5
Lunch
Cold pasta salad

Dinner
Cornish-style pasties with salad

Day 6
Lunch
Onion soup, (see page 34)

Dinner
Chicken kievs with loaded potato skins & salad

Day 7
Lunch
Egg sandwich

Dinner
Cajun chicken rice

MEAL UNDER

£2.60

EACH

RIBS IN BBQ SAUCE
with German Potato Salad

When you're on a budget, if you want to have meat you'll have to use the cheaper cuts, which means that you've got to make the tastiest meal you can with it. A perfect suggestions is these ribs that are slowly simmered, coated in delicious sweet barbeque sauce and then baked in the oven until slightly charred.

Serves 2

Ingredients for the BBQ ribs:

1 rack ribs
120g ketchup
1 tablespoon dark brown soft sugar
2 tablespoons Worcestershire sauce
1 tablespoon cider vinegar
Dash of Tabasco sauce
1 garlic clove, crushed
$^1/_2$ small onion
$^1/_4$ teaspoon English mustard
$^1/_4$ teaspoon salt
3 rings of tinned pineapple

Ingredients for the Potato Salad:

500g new potatoes or 2 medium diced potatoes
2 rashers bacon
1 tablespoon oil for frying
$^1/_2$ small onion, diced
1 tablespoon white vinegar
1 tablespoon water
$^1/_2$ teaspoon white sugar
$^1/_2$ teaspoon salt
1 teaspoon Dijon mustard
Grinding of black pepper
Small handful of chopped fresh parsley

Serve with a small mixed salad:

A few lettuce leaves
A few slices of peppers, chopped up
A few tomatoes, chopped up
Some slices of cucumber

Added options ingredients:

If you don't eat pork use turkey rashers and lamb ribs

First place your ribs in a roasting tray on the hob, and fill with water to just cover them. Bring to the boil and then simmer for 25 minutes.

While the ribs are simmering, make up your sauce by whizzing all the the BBQ ingredients with a hand blender.

Preheat the oven to 165°C. When the ribs have finished simmering, empty out the water, pat them dry and rinse and dry the roasting pan.

Put the ribs back in the pan and coat them with the sauce. Cover with foil and bake in the oven for about 40 minutes, until the meat is falling off the bone.

Meanwhile you can make the German potato salad. Pop the potatoes into a saucepan, and fill with enough water to cover and add a pinch of salt. Bring to a boil, and simmer for about 10-15 minutes, or until easily pierced with a fork. Drain, and set aside to cool.

Place the bacon in a large deep frying pan over medium-high heat, and fry with the oil until browned and crisp, turning as needed. Remove from the pan and set aside.

Add onion to the bacon grease, and cook over medium heat until browned.

Add the mustard, vinegar, water, sugar, salt and pepper to the frying pan. Turn up the heat, then add the potatoes for a couple of minutes. Crumble in half of the bacon and chopped parsley and give it a good stir through, then transfer to a serving dish. Crumble the remaining bacon over the top, and serve warm.

Serve with a small mixed salad.

slow-cooked
BEEF & ALE PIE

You don't get much more traditional British food than beef and ale pies with mash and peas. This version uses cheaper cuts of beef that are slow cooked for 4 hours to make it so tender it practically melts. As this recipe only uses 300ml of the bottled ale you can always treat yourself to a cheeky drop before dinner.

Serves 2

Ingredients for the beef & ale pie:

300g braising steak, cut into chunks and dusted in flour

1 tablespoon olive oil

2 beef stock cubes

300ml strong ale

2 teaspoons mixed herbs

1 teaspoon wholegrain mustard

4 garlic cloves, crushed

2 large onion, chopped roughly

2 large carrots, chopped into discs

3 stalks of celery, sliced

Pepper and salt, to taste

150g mushrooms

1 egg, beaten lightly, to glaze

200g of the puff pastry

3 large potatoes

Frozen peas

Added options ingredients:

Boil half a celeriac with the potatoes and mash together for a delicious alternative.

Save back 100g of the 400g braising steak for another meal. Toss the remaining 300g beef in flour and gently fry for a few minutes to caramelize the meat and add flavour.

Mix the stock cubes in a little boiling water then add to the slow cooker with the ale and herbs, give it a good stir then add the rest of the pie ingredients. Cook on low for about 4 hours until the meat is tender. Check if the seasoning is just right.

After the 4 hours are up, preheat your oven to 200°C.

To make the pies, take out half the meat with a bit of the gravy and set aside to cool for another recipe. Fill two small dish or one larger dish with the rest of the meat, vegetables and ale flavour gravy.

Brush a little egg around the top of the pie dish to help to stick the pastry.

Quickly roll out the puff pastry and sit on top of the meat, press around the edges to help it seal. You don't want to take too long as the pastry will get warm once it's in contact with the filling.

Brush over a little more egg and pop in the oven for about 20-25 minutes, until the pastry is golden. As you've not got to heat the filling it won't take as long to bake.

While the pies are cooking, peel and dice the potatoes, then boil them for about 20 minutes until soft. Drain them, then mash with butter, salt and pepper and a little grated cheese if you want.

Serve with frozen peas or any other vegetables you fancy.

MEAL UNDER
£2.60
EACH

JERK CHICKEN
with rice & black beans

I first cooked this dish a few years ago, and it's still a family favourite of ours. Sometimes I'll use the rum, but either way the rest of the flavours still work really well together. Even though you're using the cheaper legs and wings of the chicken, which are the tastier pieces, it's still important to make some cuts in the skin to let the marinade work its flavours right into the meat.

Serves 2

Ingredients for the jerk chicken:
1/2 tablespoon allspice
1/2 tablespoon black peppercorns
1 teaspoon dried chilli flakes
1/2 tablespoon sugar
2 tablespoons runny honey
A few sprigs fresh coriander, chopped
1 chilli
2 cloves garlic
1 cm piece fresh ginger, peeled
2 spring onions, trimmed and finely sliced
Drizzle of olive oil
3 tablespoons of rum or 3 tablespoons of cider vinegar
2 free-range chicken thighs, drumsticks and wings, skin on, cut a couple of slits in to the skin to help with the marinade.

Ingredients for the rice:
250g rice
2-3 spring onions, sliced
1/2 teaspoon cinnamon
600ml chicken stock
1/2 chilli
Salt and pepper
1/2 tin black beans

To serve:
Few coriander leaves scattered

Added options ingredients:
You can use frozen peas or cooked black eyed peas instead
If you don't eat pork use turkey rashers

Blitz all the jerk chicken ingredients together and marinade the chicken for a couple of hours in the fridge, or overnight if time allows.

Preheat the oven to 180°C.

Snugly place the chicken pieces in a roasting tin and pour over the marinade. Roast for about 30-45 minutes until brown and crispy

While the chicken is cooking, you can prepare the rice and beans.

Rinse the rice in plenty of cold water, refreshing it 3 times.

Drain it and tip into a large saucepan with all the remaining ingredients, except for the black beans.

Season with salt, and add 300ml cold water to boil.

When the rice starts to boil, turn down to a medium heat, cover and simmer on low for 10 minutes.

Add the black beans to the rice, turn off the heat and cover again. Leave for about 5 minutes until all the liquid is absorbed.

Serve the Jerk chicken pieces with the rice and beans, drizzle with cooked jerk sauce, then scatter over chopped coriander leaves.

BEEF RAGÙ PASTA BAKE
with fresh salad

Pasta Bake is a delicious way to enjoy pasta especially with this slow cooked beef ragù sauce. Although this dish doesn't contain much of the meat, its flavours still work well with the tomato sauce and makes a little meat go a long way. With a fresh salad and garlic dough balls you won't feel you're missing out.

Serves 2

Ingredients for the beef ragù pasta bake:

2 garlic cloves, crushed
I teaspoon dried oregano
150g mushrooms
I tablespoon olive oil
400g tinned tomatoes
150g of the slow cooked beef leftovers (see page 44)
I tablespoon tomato purée
150g dried pasta
100g grated cheese

Serve with a small mixed salad:

A few lettuce leaves
A few slices of peppers, chopped up
A few tomatoes, chopped up
Some carrots, sliced with a peeler
Some slices of cucumber

Firstly make up the ragù sauce by gently frying the garlic, oregano and mushrooms in a little oil for a few minutes then adding the tomatoes, beef and tomato purée.

Simmer on a low to medium heat for about 20 minutes until slightly reduced..

While the tomato sauce is cooking, boil then drain your pasta as per the packet instructions. Any pasta shape will do, although something like penne or twists works well.

Add the drained pasta to the sauce and give it a good stir. Tip it into an ovenproof dish and grate over the cheese. I just used Cheddar, but a bit of mozzarella would work too.

Pop in the oven for about 15 minutes until the cheese is melted and turning golden brown.

Serve with salad and maybe garlic bread or dough balls (see page 17).

MEAL UNDER
£1.50
EACH

MEAL UNDER
80p
EACH

CORNISH-STYLE PASTIES
with salad

There is nothing nicer than a Cornish pasty after a walk in the English countryside. There's a pub we sometimes visit near Swanage that only sells pasties, which is just what you want with a cold cider on a warm summers day. The twisting on the pie crust looks difficult to do, but I took a quick look online to learn how it's done.

Serves 2

Ingredients for Cornish-style pasties:
100g saved uncooked beef from page 44, finely chopped
1 medium potato, finely diced
1 carrot, finely diced
1 medium onion, finely chopped
Pinch of salt and pepper

200g puff pastry
1 egg, beaten lightly, to glaze

Added options ingredients:
You can use swede, parsnip, or peas, even sweet potato with a teaspoon of cumin

To serve:
Some pickles and a salad

Preheat the oven to 220°C

Firstly mix together the filling ingredients and season.

Roll out 2 pieces of dough on a floured surface until big enough to make a circle about 23cm across. You can use a plate to cut around.

Spoon half of the filling on to one half of each pastry circle, leaving a a good margin for crimping.

Brush round the edge with beaten egg. or water.

Now fold over the empty semicircle of pastry and and stick it down about 1cm short of the bottom edge. This is for the crimp.

You now fold that edge back over the top layer and crimp it with your finger.

Carefully lift onto a nonstick baking tray and brush with the egg to glaze.

Bake for 10 minutes, then lower the temperature to 170°C and cook for another 30 minutes until golden brown. Cover with a layer of foil if it looks like it's browning a little too quickly.

Serve with some pickles and a salad to make you feel a bit less guilty.

CHICKEN KIEVS
with loaded potato skins & salad

I looked up the original recipe for chicken kievs and it seems that they don't come from the Ukraine capital after all. They came from the French chefs that worked for the wealthy Russian households that later moved over to New York, where some of restaurants trying to please Russian immigrants gave chicken supreme the name kiev. Which then came back to Europe again just to confuse us all!

Serves 2

Ingredients for the chicken Kievs:

1-2 cloves garlic, crushed and chopped
small handful of parsley, chopped
2 teaspoons softened butter
2 free-range chicken breasts
4 bacon rashers, thinned
50g flour
Salt and pepper
1 egg
2 crusts for bread crumbs
2 tablespoons olive oil

Ingredients for the loaded potato skins:

2 large potatoes
1 bacon rasher, chopped
80g grated cheese
1/2 chopped onion
1/2 teaspoon Dijon or wholegrain mustard

Serve with a small mixed salad:

A few lettuce leaves
A few slices of red and yellow peppers, chopped up
A few tomatoes, chopped up
Some carrots, sliced with a peeler
Some slices of cucumber

Added options ingredients:

If you don't eat pork use turkey rashers

Preheat the oven to 200°C.

While you have the oven on it's a good idea to cook a couple of potatoes for lunches later in the week.

To cook the chicken kievs, firstly make the garlic butter by mixing the crushed garlic with the butter and finely chopped parsley stalks and leaves

Take off the extra bits of chicken fillets for the Cajun rice later in the week. Cut a slice on the underside of one of the chicken breasts, being careful not to cut right through. Fill this with the garlic butter and close it up to seal in the mixture.

Lay 2 rashers of bacon on a clean cutting board and stretch out with the back of a knife to thin out. Lay the chicken breast on top and roll the bacon around it. This should help enclose the butter even more.

In 3 separate bowls add a little flour with salt and pepper, an egg with a dash of water, mixed with a fork and some prepared bread crumbs.

Dip the bacon wrapped chicken in the flour, then the egg mixture, then the bread crumbs. Then fry for a few minutes in a little olive oil, turning once until the crumb coating is golden. Repeat with the second chicken breast.

Finish cooking in the oven with the potatoes for another 10-15 minutes until the chicken is white and cooked through.

Serve with the loaded jacket potato skins (see page 150) and a small salad.

MEAL UNDER
£2.50
EACH

CAJUN CHICKEN RICE

This rice dish makes a change from the usual stirfry I'd make at the end of the week to use up the last of the meat and veg. With the spicy cayenne pepper and tabasco sauce it doesn't feel like a leftovers meal, but that's what makes cheaper recipes from around the world just so good. Some of the tastiest dishes originate from the necessity of feeding yourself on a very small budget.

Serves 2 with leftovers

Ingredients for the Cajun chicken rice:
200g long grain rice
1 tablespoon cooking oil
2 bacon rashers, thinly chopped
2 small saved free-range chicken fillets, diced
2 bay leaves
$1/2$ medium onion, finely chopped
$1/2$ green pepper, finely chopped
2 stalks of celery, finely chopped
Pinch of salt and pepper
2 teaspoons cayenne pepper
2 garlic cloves, finely chopped
$1/2$ tin black beans
Splash of tabasco sauce
Parsley, to finish
Squeeze of lemon juice (optional)

Added options ingredients:
You can use frozen peas or cooked kidney beans or black eyed peas instead..
If you don't eat pork use turkey rashers instead

Cook the rice according to the packet instructions.

Put the oil in a pan and heat up. Cook the bacon for a few minutes, then add your chicken and cook until slightly golden.

Add the bay leaves and then onion, peppers and celery. Season with the salt, pepper and the cayenne pepper.

Once the vegetables have softened, add the garlic and cook for a few more minutes. Next add the black beans and cook for a further 5 minutes, then add the rice and tabasco and stir together until heated through.

Serve with a little squeeze of lemon and sprinkle of the parsley.

You can add a little more tabasco if you want it a bit more spicy.

MEAL UNDER £1 EACH

WEEK 2

1	2 loaves sliced wholemeal bread	**11**	2.5kg potatoes
2	Olive spread	**12**	Fresh parsley
3	Salted butter	**13**	2 x carrots
4	250g Cheddar cheese	**14**	Red cabbage
5	1 whole free-range chicken	**15**	2 x limes
6	Garlic	**16**	Chillies
7	Ginger	**17**	Little gem lettuce
8	1kg onions	**18**	Packet of 3 peppers
9	1 x 400g tin tomatoes	**19**	Packet of 6 tomatoes
10	1 x 400ml tin coconut milk	**20**	1 cucumber

21	Celery	**31**	Fresh coriander
22	400g skinless salmon	**32**	Broccoli
23	200g smoked haddock	**33**	500g pasta
24	225g prawns	**34**	1kg rice
25	4 pints of milk	**35**	Lemongrass
26	12 free-range eggs	**36**	200g chorizo
27	1kg frozen peas	**37**	Desiccated coconut
28	1.5g plain flour		
29	500g natural yogurt		
30	Brioche buns		

Shopping list for lunch and dinner for 2 for 7 days

DAY-BY-DAY
MENU FOR WEEK 2

This week is more fishy, and I don't mean it's suspicious. I've used salmon, haddock and prawns to create some lovely traditional and interesting meals you'll want to cook again and again. I also use free-range chicken that stretches to three meals including a Thai red curry that's full of flavour and heat.

There's also a jambalaya from the deep south of America and some Caribbean-style coconut prawns. For a more traditional flavour I've added good old fish pie and a simple salmon pasta dish.

Day 1
Lunch
Pea soup

Dinner
Chicken burger with homemade coleslaw

Day 2
Lunch
Cheese and coleslaw sandwich

Dinner
Fish pie

Day 3
Lunch
Leftover fish pie

Dinner
Coconut prawns with rice

Day 4
Lunch
Egg salad sandwich

Dinner
Jambalaya

Day 5
Lunch
Leftover Jambalaya

Dinner
Chorizo omelette with potato wedges & coleslaw salad

Day 6
Lunch
Egg sandwich

Dinner
Salmon pasta bake with broccoli

Day 7
Lunch
Leftover salmon pasta bake

Dinner
Thai red chicken curry with rice

CHICKEN FILLET BURGER
with homemade coleslaw

We all like the odd takeaway, and the high street being full of chicken shops shows the type of food we enjoy the most. But it can be expensive to keep buying takeaways, and if like me you're interested in the welfare of your food, you will appriciate this version cooked at home. This is a quick and easy chicken burger that's just as tasty as that well-know brand, even if their ingredients are supposedly secret.

Serves 2

Ingredients for the chicken burger:
2 free-range chicken breasts, flattened
½ tablespoon ground cumin
½ tablespoon smoked paprika
½ tablespoon ground coriander
Pinch of salt and pepper
3 tablespoons plain flour
1 egg, beaten
1 crust of bread made into fine bread crumbs

Ingredients for the coleslaw:
1 large carrot, grated
¼ red cabbage, shredded
4 tablespoons Greek yogurt
4 tablespoons mayonnaise
Pinch of salt and pepper
Juice of ½ lime

Few lettuce leaves, shredded
2 brioche buns

Added options ingredients:
You could add crispy bacon or melt some cheese on the chicken fillets during the last minute of cooking

To make the coleslaw, firstly grate the carrot into a large bowl and mix together with the shredded red cabbage, yogurt mayonnaise, salt and pepper and squeeze of lime juice.

Take off the mini fillet from the inside of the breast, and cut the pointy end of the chicken to make it a bit more square. These pieces will be saved in the fridge for the curry later in the week.

Next flatten the chicken breasts, by putting them between 2 sheets of greaseproof paper and giving them a good bash with a rolling pin until they are about 1cm thick.

Using 3 shallow bowls, pop the flour in one, beat an egg with a touch of water, in the next. In the third, mix the bread crumbs with the spices and stir well.

One by one dip the coated chicken pieces in the flour, then the egg mixture, then the bread crumbs and fry in a shallow pan for about 10 minutes, turning half way through until golden, checking that they are cooked right the way through.

Heat up a griddle if you have one, or toast under a grill the insides of the split brioche buns.

Now you're ready to build your delicious burgers.

On the bottom layer spread a tablespoon of mayonnaise, then a layer of shredded lettuce. Next lay the chicken fillet and top of with the coleslaw and toasted brioche lid.

Serve with potato wedges or salad if you want.

Save half the coleslaw for later in the week.

MEAL UNDER

£2.70

EACH

FISH PIE
with crunchy cheese topping

This fish pie is a real favourite in our house. We've been cooking it forever. When the nights start drawing in, it's a tasty warming treat to look forward to. You can uses any fish, but it's best for one of them to be smoked to add a depth of flavour. I've also used a few chopped prawns in this version, but feel free to leave them out.

Serves 2 with leftovers

Ingredients for the fish pie:
200g skinless salmon fillet
200g smoked haddock fillet
40g raw prawns, halved

400ml milk
1 small onion, quartered
4 cloves
2 bay leaves
2 eggs
150g frozen peas
25g butter
25g plain flour
500g potato, peeled and cut into
even-sized chunks
25g Cheddar cheese, grated
Pinch of ground nutmeg

Serve with steamed broccoli if you like

Preheat the oven to 200°C.

Boil the potatoes for 20 minutes until soft, then drain and season. Mash with a knob of the butter and a drop of milk.

Next poach the fish, by putting it in a frying pan and pour over 200ml of the milk. Poke each onion quarter with a clove, then add to the milk, with the bay leaves.

Bring the milk just to the boil, then reduce to a simmer for 8 minutes. Lift the fish onto a plate and strain the milk through a sieve into a jug.

Flake the fish into bite size pieces and pop in a baking dish, with the peas.

Hard-boil 2 eggs for about 6-8 minutes. Then drain and cool in cold running water. Peel the eggs and slice into quarters, then add to the fish and peas.

To make the white sauce, first melt the butter in a pan, stir in the flour and cook for 1 minute over a low heat. Take the pan off the heat and pour in a some of the poaching milk, stirring until blended.

Keep adding the milk gradually and mixing well until the sauce is smooth. Return to the heat, then bring to the boil for 5 minutes, still stirring, until it coats the back of a wooden spoon. If it gets too thick, whisk harder and add a touch more milk.

Take off the heat and season with salt, pepper and nutmeg, then pour over the fish mixture. Spoon over the mash, ruff the top with a fork and sprinkle over with cheese, Bake in the oven for about for 30 minutes until its crunchy on top and piping hot.

MEAL UNDER
£2
EACH

COCONUT PRAWNS
with rice & spicy dipping sauce

When I first made this dish, I used chillies I'd slow grown on my window sill. Wow were they hot! Therefore I've only suggested one chilli in the dip, but feel free to add more if you want to. The coconut flavour of the prawn bread crumbs adds a delicious Caribbean flavour that works well with the spicy dipping sauce.

Serves 2

Ingredients for the coconut prawns:
145g defrosted raw peeled prawns

Ingredients for the batter
150g plain flour, plus 1 tablespoon
1 teaspoon baking powder
$^1/_2$ teaspoon paprika
200ml water
60g bread crumbs
60g desiccated coconut
Pinch of black pepper
$^1/_2$ teaspoon of salt
Vegetable/rapeseed oil, for deep frying

Ingredients for the spicy dipping sauce:
1 chilli, roughly chopped
1 onion, roughly chopped
1 garlic clove
3 tablespoons white wine vinegar
$^1/_2$ teaspoon ground ginger
Juice of $^1/_2$ lime
$^1/_2$ teaspoon ground allspice
$^1/_2$ teaspoon salt
1 tablespoon sugar
coriander, to scatter (optional)

Ingredients for the rice:
1 cup of rice to 2 cups of water
Pinch of salt

Firstly make your dipping sauce by whizzing all the ingredients with a blender until fairly smooth. Pour this into a saucepan and bring to the boil, simmer for about 5 minutes, then let it cool down.

For the batter, mix the flour with the baking powder and a pinch of salt in a bowl, make a well in centre and add in the water, then whisk to make a smooth batter.

In another bowl mix a tablespoon of flour with the bread crumbs, salt, pepper, paprika and coconut, then tip half on to a baking tray and shake to spread out.

Dip the prawns into the batter. Then, one at a time, shake them a little before laying them out in the coconut crumb mixture, and sprinkle over the rest of the mixture, coating well. Leave them in the tray while you prepare the rice and heat up the oil.

Before you start to fry the prawns, cook your rice by firstly rinsing it in cold water, then in a saucepan pour twice as much water as rice, add a pinch of salt, then put the lid on and bring to the boil. Simmer for about 10 minutes. You'll know when it's ready as the surface of the rice will be dimpled.

In a deep saucepan heat up 5cm of oil, so that a cube of bread should turn brown in one minute when dropped in.

Deep-fry the prawns a few at a time for 1-2 minutes until golden-brown and crisp, then drain on kitchen paper.

Serve with the rice, a pot of the dipping sauce and maybe some lime wedges and a scatter of spring onions and chilli if you want.

JAMBALAYA

I first tried Jambalaya at a street festival in New Orleans years ago, and have found some great recipes out there. It's perfect for a budget recipe book or blog as the whole idea of it stems from trying to make a few ingredients go a long way in the tastiest way you can. We sometimes make a huge pan of it and freeze it for delicious mid-week meals towards the end of the month.

Serves 2 with leftovers

Ingredients for the Jamblaya:
2 free-range chicken legs, divided into drumsticks and thighs, plus the wings for flavour
250g rice
1 tablespoon oil
1 onion, diced
1 red pepper, diced
1 green pepper, diced
1 stick of celery (optional)
2 bay leaves (optional)
2 garlic cloves, crushed
100g sliced chorizo
1 tablespoon cayenne pepper
Pinch of salt and pepper
400g tinned tomatoes
350ml chicken stock
1 chilli
40g raw prawns, halved
Handful of chopped parsley

Season the chicken with salt, pepper and the cayenne.

Pour oil into a large saucepan and brown the chicken pieces over a medium heat.

After 5 minutes add the chorizo. Once nicely browned on all sides, add your onion, peppers and celery as well as your bay leaves and another pinch of salt and pepper.

Stir, then fry on a medium heat for 10-12 minutes, stirring every now and again.

Once the vegetables have softened, add your garlic and chillies, stir around for a minute, then stir in the tinned tomatoes and chicken stock.

Bring everything to the boil, then turn the heat down, put the lid on the pan and simmer for 25-30 minutes.

When you can pull the meat off the bone and shred it easily, the chicken's ready. Feel free to remove the chicken skin and bones at this point if you like, then add your rice.

Give it all a good stir, then put the lid on. Give it a stir every few minutes so it doesn't stick to the base of the pan.

Let it cook for about 15-20 minutes until the rice is cooked. Stir in the prawns and if it needs it, add enough water to make it a kind of porridgey consistency.

Put the lid back on and cook for another 3-4 minutes to cook the prawns, while you chop the parsley. Stir the parsley through, check the seasoning and serve.

MEAL UNDER
£1
EACH

CHORIZO OMELET
with Potato wedges & colesla

We normally always have a few eggs in the fridge, so a quick and easy om
if the trains are playing up or we're working late. For this one I used a few
tomatoes from the garden, but any variation is fine – just remember to de-
ones so the omelette isn't sloppy.

Serves 2

Ingredients for the omelette:
100g chorizo, cut in to 5mm slices
A few baby tomatoes halved, or a large one
de-seeded and diced
4 eggs, beaten
Knob of butter
Salt and pepper
A few springs of thyme leaves, or $^1/_2$ teaspoon of dried
30g grated cheese

Ingredients for the potato wedges:
2 medium potatoes
2 tablespoons cooking oil
Pinch of salt

To serve:
Red cabbage coleslaw (see page 60)

Firstly slice the potatoes into wedges, toss in a tray with a little oil and a pinch of salt, then put in the oven for 25-30 minutes, turning them halfway through.

Heat an ovenproof frying pan with the butter, add the sliced chorizo, and cook for a few minutes to release the oils from the sausage. Then add the tomato and the thyme leaves, and gently fry for another 6-8 minutes until softened.

Meanwhile crack the eggs in to a bowl, add salt and pepper and beat well with a fork.

Put the grill on. If it's in the same oven like mine, move the potato wedges to the bottom rung.

Add the eggs to the chorizo mixture and stir around a bit until the eggs start to firm up.

Cook the underside of the omelette for a couple of minutes, then scatter over the cheese.

Pop the pan under the grill for a few minutes until puffed up, golden and the cheese has melted.

Serve with potato wedges and a red cabbage coleslaw, (see page 60).

MEAL UNDER
£1.50
EACH

SALMON PASTA BAKE
with broccoli

This has been a family favourite since my daughter was little. It's still one of her favourites and now she makes it herself. Any pasta shape will work, but these twisted fusilli ones are great for holding on to more delicious sauce per fork full.

Serves 2 with leftovers

Ingredients for the pasta bakep:

200g of the salmon, chopped in to 1-inch pieces
1/2 the broccoli head, chopped in to 1-inch pieces and blanched for a couple of minutes in boiling water.
1 tomato, sliced, for the top
150g pasta
white sauce
Cheddar cheese, grated for the topping

Ingredients for the white sauce:

20g unsalted butter
20g plain flour
300ml milk
1/2 teaspoon of Dijon mustard
75g Cheddar cheese, grated

Added options ingredients:

We sometimes add quartered boiled eggs to the fish and broccoli too.

Firstly cook your pasta as per the packet instructions.

Preheat the oven to 190°C, and boil the kettle.

Skin the fish, then feel for, and take out any bones that may still be attached. Cut your fish into bite-size pieces.

Chop the broccoli into bite-size florets, place in a saucepan with a pinch of salt and pour over boiling water. Bring back to the boil and simmer for about 2 minutes. Drain and scatter with the salmon into a deep casserole dish.

To make the white sauce, first melt the butter in a pan, then stir in the flour and cook for 1 minute over a low heat.

Take the pan off the heat and pour in some of the milk, stirring until blended.

Keep adding the milk gradually and mixing well until the sauce is smooth. Return to a gentle heat, then bring to the boil for 5 minutes still stirring. Add 50g of cheese and the mustard and mix well.

Pour the drained pasta into the white cheesy sauce and stir well, then lay this on top of the fish and broccoli. Scatter over the remaining cheese and sliced tomatoes and a grind of black pepper to finish .

Cook in the oven for about 30 minutes or until heated right through and crunchy on top.

THAI RED CHICKEN CURRY
with rice

We all know about Thai green curry, and I've even got a recipe in my other book for a vegan version. But this Thai red curry will knock your socks off. It's not just hot, it's full of flavour. If you're not keen on spicy food, maybe leave out a chilli or two, but I prefer mine to make my mouth go numb.

Serves 2

Ingredients for the red curry paste:
2 teaspoons ground cumin
2 teaspoons ground coriander
4 red chillies, roughly chopped
1 tablespoon paprika
2 lemongrass stalks, roughly chopped
4cm piece fresh ginger, chopped
The finely grated zest of 1 lime
1 medium onion, chopped
5 garlic cloves, chopped
Stalks from a small bunch of fresh coriander
2 tablespoons fish sauce
2 tablespoons vegetable oil

Ingredients for the Thai red curry:
60g desiccated coconut
1 tablespoon vegetable oil
2 garlic cloves, crushed
Half thumb-sized piece ginger, cut into matchsticks
4 tablespoons of the red curry paste
400ml coconut milk
Mini free-range chicken fillets, and the extra bits diced
$^1/_2$ red cabbage, shredded thinly
$^1/_2$ green pepper, sliced
$^1/_2$ red pepper, sliced
1 onion, sliced
1 tablespoon fish sauce
$^1/_2$ teaspoon brown sugar
Coriander leaves saved, plus extra to serve
1 red chilli, sliced diagonally

1 cup rice
$^1/_2$ lime
Small amount of chopped coriander

Firstly make the red curry paste beforehand. It can be saved in a clean jar in the fridge for up to a week.

Whizz everything into a smooth paste in a food processor or hand blender.

Next cook the rice as per the instructions on page 21

Toast the coconut in a dry pan for a few minutes until it starts to turn golden brown. Tip out onto a plate and wipe the saucepan so you can cook the rest of the curry.

Fry the onions, peppers, ginger and garlic in the pan with the oil for 10 minutes or so, then add the red curry paste, and let it sizzle for a few seconds before pouring in the coconut milk.

Bring to the boil then reduce to a simmer.

Add the cabbage and chicken and let it simmer for about 15 minutes until the chicken is cooked through.

Add the fish sauce and the brown sugar, then taste. Add more fish sauce if you like it salty or a little more sugar if sweeter.

Bring to the boil, take off the heat and stir through the toasted coconut and some chopped coriander.

Spoon the curry into 2 bowls with the rice, and top with 1 sliced red chilli, and a little more of the extra coriander leaves and a lime wedge.

MEAL UNDER
£2.50
EACH

①	2 loaves sliced wholemeal bread		⑫	Chillies
②	Olive spread		⑬	Fresh coriander
③	Salted butter		⑭	Fresh parsley
④	2 pints of milk		⑮	Fresh mint
⑤	12 free-range eggs		⑯	1.5kg strong flour
⑥	400g paneer		⑰	500g natural yogurt
⑦	300g fresh spinach		⑱	3 courgettes
⑧	1 × 400g tin chickpeas		⑲	250g Cheddar cheese
⑨	1 × 400g tin kidney beans		⑳	250g feta cheese/Greek
⑩	1kg white onions		㉑	White cabbage
⑪	Ginger		㉒	300g mushrooms

WEEK 3

23	500g penne pasta	34	100g jar chipotle paste
24	Little gem lettuce	35	1 x 400g tin tomatoes
25	Radishes	36	1kg rice
26	Packet of 3 peppers	37	1kg frozen peas
27	1.5kg plain flour	38	200g packet of cashews
28	4 carrots	39	Packet of 6 pitta breads
29	1 cucumber	40	50g miso soup paste
30	1kg sweet potatoes	41	1kg red onions
31	2 lemons	42	Garlic
32	1 lime	43	Packet of 6 tomatoes
33	153g jar pitted olives		Shopping list for lunch and dinner for 2 for 7 days

DAY-BY-DAY VEGETARIAN
MENU FOR WEEK 3

Just because it's a budget vegetarian week, doesn't mean you'll have to live on kale and nut cutlets. There's plenty of intresting dishes to try that'll show that you don't need to eat meat every week. We often go weeks at a time not eating it ourselves and don't even realise.

There's plenty of flavour this week with Mexican rice or Middle Eastern falafal pitta pockets, as well as Indian paneer curry, Japanese gyoza or Italian garlic dough balls. It's like a culinary world cruise for vegetarians.

Day 1
Lunch
Cheese on toast

Dinner
Paneer & spinach curry with naan breads

Day 2
Lunch
Sweet potato soup, (see page 35)

Dinner
Courgette & feta rosti with coleslaw salad

Day 3
Lunch
Cheese and coleslaw sandwich

Dinner
Paneer & vegetable skewers with sweet potato wedges and Greek salad

Day 4
Lunch
Egg salad sandwich

Dinner
Mexican-style rice

Day 5
Lunch
Leftover Mexican-style rice

Dinner
Courgette pasta carbonara with garlic dough balls & salad

Day 6
Lunch
Leftover pasta

Dinner
Chickpea falafels with pitta pockets, dips and salad

Day 7
Lunch
Pitta, hummus and salad with miso soup

Dinner
Vegetable gyoza with a Japanese-style salad & dressing

PANEER & SPINACH CURRY
with naan breads

Paneer is a great substitute for meat if you're trying a vegetarian week like we do every now and then. It works really well with this dish, as it soaks up all the delicious curry spices and goes lovely and crispy on the edges. I've teamed it with a homemade naan bread that's so easy to make, but if you're unsure, I have provided an easy-to-follow cooking video on my FoodologistGirl YouTube channel.

Serves 2 with extra naans

Ingredients for the naan dough:
1 teaspoon quick yeast
1 teaspoon caster sugar
$1/2$ teaspoon salt
300g strong flour, plus extra for rolling
1 tablespoon olive oil
150ml natural yogurt
25g melted butter

Ingredients for the curry:
1 tablespoon butter
$1/2$ teaspoon turmeric
$1/2$ teaspoon chilli powder
200g x paneer, cut into cubes
300g fresh spinach
1 400g tin chickpeas
1 onion, finely chopped
1 garlic clove finely chopped
Thumb-sized piece of ginger, finely chopped
1 chilli, finely sliced
$1/2$ teaspoon turmeric
$1/2$ teaspoon chilli powder
1 teaspoon garam masala
chopped coriander, to serve

To make the naans, (see page 14)

For the curry, in a large frying pan with a lid, melt the butter, stir in the spices, then add the cubed paneer and mix well.

Fry for about 6-8 minutes until golden and just starting to crisp on the ends. Keep turning to cook each side.

Take out the paneer and set aside. Over a medium heat cook the onions, garlic, ginger and chilli in the flavoured butter. for about 10 minutes until the onion is starting to soften

Add the chickpeas and cook for another 5-6 minutes with the lid on to heat through, then add about 100ml of water to release all the flavours from the bottom of the pan.

Give the chickpeas a little squash with a potato masher, but not too much, you just want to mash about half of them. Put the lid on and cook for another few minutes.

Now turn down the heat and add the spinach with another good splash of water and put the lid back on while it wilts for about 5 minutes.

Once wilted give it a good stir. Make sure it's not too watery. If so, cook for a little longer, then add the paneer.

Cook for a couple more minutes to warm through the cheese then serve with the chopped coriander, natural yogurt and your naan breads.

COURGETTE & FETA ROSTI
with coleslaw salad

I never used to like shop-bought coleslaw growing up, but having tasted my friend's homemade version I now realise the stuff you buy in the shops is a million miles away from that. I've added mustard to my recipe to give it a kick, and it complements the crunchy feta fritters perfectly.

Serves 2

Ingredients for the rosti:
1 ½ courgettes
1 lemon zest only, the juice will be used later in the week
1 red chilli, finely chopped
A small bunch of fresh mint, finely chopped
1 egg, beaten
25g plain flour
20g grated cheddar cheese
Pinch of dried oregano or mixed herbs
100g feta, or Greek salad cheese
2-3 tablespoons of olive oil, to shallow fry

Ingredients for the coleslaw:
1 medium onion
½ small white cabbage
1 large carrot
1 heaped teaspoon Dijon mustard
4 tablespoons mayonnaise
2 tablespoons natural yogurt
Salt and pepper, to taste
A little chopped parsley, if you have it.

Firstly coarsely grate the courgette and pat dry to remove excess water. You don't want it soggy.

Next, in a bowl, combine the grated courgette with the flour and grated cheese, the herbs, the chilli, lemon zest, seasoning and beaten egg.

Mix it all up with your hands, then crumble in the feta and mix that in.

Divide in to six then shape into balls and flatten.

Heat a non-stick frying pan over a medium heat and add the oil. Fry the rosti for 2-3 minutes on each side until golden brown.

For the coleslaw, thinly slice the cabbage and grate the onion and carrot.

Mix together with the mayonnaise, yogurt and mustard then season to taste and mix the parsley if using.

There will be more coleslaw than you need, but it goes great in cheese sandwiches for your lunch..

PANEER & VEGETABLE SKEWERS
with sweet potato wedges & Greek salad

Paneer doesn't have to be just for curries. As it's similar to halloumi but a little cheaper, you can use it in Mediterranean-style recipes too, like these roast vegetable skewers with sweet potatoes and Greek salad. Just the sort of dish you could get from a Greek taverna on Skiathos.

Serves 2

Ingredients for the skewers:
200g paneer cheese, cut into cubes
1 red pepper, cut into small chunks
1/2 courgette, cut into 5mm slices
2-3 mushrooms, quartered
Handful of cherry tomatoes

Ingredients for the marinade:
A small bunch of fresh mint, finely chopped
1 fresh red chilli, finely chopped
1 lemon
2 tablespoons olive oil
Salt and pepper

Ingredients for the sweet potato chips:
2 medium sweet potatoes
2 tablespoons of oil
Salt

Ingredients for the Greek-style salad:
1 small red onion, finely sliced
3 inches of cucumber, sliced
2 tomatoes, cut into chunks
A handful of olives
50g feta or Greek salad cheese, broken over
Drizzle of extra virgin olive oil
Salt and pepper

Firstly mix all the marinade ingredients together and marinade the cubed paneer cheese for at least 1 hour in the fridge.

Next cut up the vegetables and stick them onto skewers along with the cheese in a random fashion.

Lay them on a baking sheet and drizzle some of the marinade over them.

Preheat the oven to 200°C.

Slice the sweet potatoes lengthways into wedges. You should get about 6-8 per potato.

Drizzle over the oil and salt, then with your hands give it a good mix, coating the potatoes all over.

Put in the oven and cook for about 25-30 minutes, turning after 15 minutes.

When you put the sweet potatoes in, you can put the skewers in too.

Bake in the oven for about 15 minutes then turn them around and drizzle over some more of the marinade. Cook for a further 15 minutes until they are just golden around the edges.

While the potatoes and skewers are cooking, make up the salad by mixing all the ingredients together then scattering the feta cheese and drizzling the oil over.

Serve with the salad and sweet potato wedges. and a dollop of natural yogurt if you have it in the fridge

MEXICAN-STYLE RICE
with broken feta

I'm a recent convert to chipotle paste, and I'd have it in most recipes if I could. It really brings a simple dish like rice to life with colour and flavour. I added carrots, peas and kidney beans to this to bulk it out a bit more, so there'll be plenty for leftovers, if you don't eat it all in one go.

Serves 2 with leftovers

Ingredients for the Mexican rice:
1 tablespoon oil
1/2 x 400g tin kidney beans
1 red onion, finely chopped
2 teaspoons chipotle paste
1 carrot, finely sliced
1 x 400g tin tomatoes
150g rice
100g frozen peas
3-4 mushrooms, quartered
Zest and juice of 1 lime
Handful of sultanas (optional)
Salt and pepper to taste
Handful of crushed cashews (optional)
100g feta of Greek salad cheese, to scatter
Coriander, to scatter

Firstly wash the rice a few times until the water runs clear, and drain.

In a saucepan fry the onions for about 5 minutes on a medium heat, then add the carrots and cook for another 5 minutes.

Add the rice and chipotle paste and cook for a minute, stirring it to coat everything.

Next add the tin chopped tomatoes, then fill the tin with cold water and add that too.

Bring to the boil and add the frozen peas, kidney beans and mushrooms, then turn down to a simmer with the lid on and cook for another 10 minutes, checking once or twice.

Check to see if it needs more water or cooking for longer, then add the sultanas and lime. Season with salt and pepper.

Serve with broken pieces of feta, crushed cashews and chopped coriander.

MEAL UNDER
£1.30
EACH

COURGETTE PASTA CARBONARA
with garlic dough balls & salad

If you're on a budget, you don't need to miss out on your favourite restaurant's garlic dough balls. Make your own with this easy recipe, that goes perfect with salad and this tasty courgette and mushroom carbonara. They're very garlicky so just make sure you're both eating them.

Serves 2 with leftovers

Ingredients for the pasta:
3-4 mushrooms sliced or quartered
1 courgette baton, sliced
2 cloves garlic
4 egg yokes
250g penne pasta, some saved for lunch
50g grated cheddar cheese
1 tablespoon olive oil
Salt and pepper, to taste

Ingredients for the dough balls:
250g strong white bread flour
$1/2$ teaspoon salt
$1/2$ teaspoon sugar
7g butter, softened
$1/2$ teaspoon quick yeast
150ml warm water

Ingredients for the garlic butter:
1 tablespoon butter, softened
1 tablepoon oil
2 garlic cloves, crushed
Handful of parsley, finely chopped

Serve with a small mixed salad:
A few lettuce leaves
A few slices of peppers, chopped up
A few tomatoes chopped up
Some carrots sliced with a peeler
Some slices of cucumber

Firstly put some salted water in a large pan on to boil for the pasta.

Cook the penne according to the packet instructions.

While the pasta is cooking heat the oil in a deep sided frying pan, and gently fry the mushrooms, garlic and courgettes for about 10 minutes until softened.

While the vegetables are cooking, in a bowl mix with a fork the cheese with the eggs yokes. Season with salt and pepper. (Save the whites for meringue on page 191).

When the pasta is cooked, drain it over a bowl and keep back a little of the starchy water.

Pour the cooked pasta into the courgette and mushroom mixture and stir.

Turn off the pan and wait a minute for it to cool a touch, then pour in the egg mixture and give it all a good stir. You don't want the eggs to scramble but you do want them to cook in the heat of the pasta.

Add a little of the saved water if it's a bit dry to loosen it slightly.

Taste and add more ground pepper and cheese if you like.

Serve with a salad and the garlic dough balls (see page 17 for the method).

CHICKPEA FALAFELS
with pitta pockets, dips and salad

When I started my budget recipe blog over 3 years ago, this was one of the first recipes I cooked, mainly because it's so cheap, nutritious and tasty. The homemade falafels are from budget tins of chickpeas and kidney beans – and as they get mashed anyway who cares? Homemade hummus and tzatziki turns this into another delicious Mediterranean meal.

Serves 2

Ingredients for the falafels:
$1/2$ x 400g tin chickpeas
$1/2$ 400g x tin kidney beans
1 heaped teaspoon allspice
1 tablespoon plain flour
Juice of half a lemon
Few stalks of fresh coriander, finely chopped
Salt and pepper, to taste

2 large pittas, cut in half

Ingredients for the tzatziki:
2 tablespoons Greek yogurt
6cm cucumber
1 garlic clove, crushed
$1/2$ tablespoon olive oil
Squeeze of lemon juice
Handful of fresh mint leaves, finely chopped
Pinch of salt and pepper

Ingredients for the hummus:
$1/2$ x 400g tin chickpeas
2 tablespoons lemon juice
2 garlic cloves, crushed
1 teaspoon ground cumin
Pinch of salt
1 tablespoon tahini (sesame seed paste) (optional)
4 tablespoons water
1 tablespoon extra virgin olive oil

Serve with a few lettuce leaves, chopped up baby tomatoes, some slices of red onion, some slices of cucumber

To make the tzatziki, cut the cucumber in half and scoop out and discard the seeds.

Grate the cucumber, pat the excess water off with a paper towel and mix into the yogurt with the rest of the ingredients and season to taste.

To make the hummus, drain the chickpeas. You need half the tin for the humus and the other half for the falafels. Rinse.them and reserve a few whole chickpeas for serving.

Combine all the ingredients except the oil in a food processor, and blend to a purée. If you can't get hold of tahini paste, leave it out. I have before and it's fine.

Add more lemon juice, cumin or salt to taste and drizzle a little oil over the hummus before serving. along with the resevved whole chickpeas.

To make the falafels, pop in a bowl the drained kidney beans, and chickpeas with the coriander, lemon, all spice, flour, salt and pepper.

Blend until smooth, either with a fork or food processor, then divide and shape into 6-8 small patties.

Put 1 tablespoon of oil into a pan and shallow fry the falafels until crisp and golden.

Serve with toasted pitta breads, sliced in half and opened into pockets, with salad and the dips. Open them carefully when hot or they'll crack once they cool down.

MEAL UNDER
75p
EACH

VEGETABLE GYOZA
with a Japanese-style salad and dressing

These might look complicated to make, but really they're not that fiddly. I made my own pastry wrappers, and there's a recipe below for that, but most large supermarkets also sell them. The spicy tomato dressing is for dipping the gyoza in, but also perfect for dressing the salad.

Serves 2

Ingredients for the gyoza pastry wrappers:
1 egg
$1/2$ teaspoon salt
200g plain flour
50ml water

Ingredients for the gyoza filling:
3 garlic cloves, crushed
1 x 2cm piece of ginger
1 fresh red chilli
$1/2$ small onion
1 carrot
2-3 mushrooms
100g white cabbage
1 teaspoon sesame oil
2 teaspoons miso paste
2 teaspoons soy sauce

Ingredients for the Japanese-style salad:
A few lettuce leaves
A few radishes, sliced
1 carrot, thinly sliced
A few thin slices of cucumber
1 chilli, thinly sliced
1 spring onion, thinly sliced (optional)

Ingredients for the Japanese dressing:
1 tablespoon of rice wine or white wine vinegar
1 tablespoon soy sauce
1 teaspoon caster sugar
$1/2$ small onion, finely chopped
1 teaspoon grated ginger
$1/2$ tablespoon tomato purée
1 tablespoon vegetable oil

You can buy the gyoza pastry wrappers from most big supermarkets, but they're quite easy to make. Just mix the dry ingredients together, then add the egg, then the water and make into a dough as you would pasta (see page 18). Roll out and using a large 9-10cm cookie cutter.

For the gyoza filling, put all the ingredients in a food processor and blitz until a rough paste.

To make up the gyoza, have a small bowl of water next to you, and a lightly cornfloured surface to stop them sticking.

Take one of the gyoza pasty circles and put a teaspoon of filling into the middle. Brush the edges with a little water, then fold the wrapper in half over the filling to make a half circle shape.

Pinch and pleat the edges to seal, as the photo shows and place on the floured surface. Repeat until either the pastry circles have run out or the ingredients. You should make about 16.

Next heat up 1 tablespoon of oil in a large lidded non-stick frying pan and cook the gyoza in a single layer, flat side down for a minute, then reduce to medium heat for about 2 minutes until the underside is golden.

Carefully pour 1cm of water into the pan and immediately cover with a lid and steam the gyoza for about 5-6 minutes or until most of the water evaporates.

Take off the lid and cook uncovered until the gyoza is nice and crisp on the bottom. Add a little more oil if needed.

Serve with the salad and dressing. To make the Japanese salad dressing simply put all the ingredients in a clean jam jar and give it a good shake.

1	2 loaves sliced wholemeal bread	11	3 x lemons
2	Olive spread	12	Garlic
3	Salted butter	13	250g cream cheese
4	2 pints of milk	14	250g Cheddar cheese
5	12 free-range eggs	15	Fresh sage leaves
6	200g feta/Greek cheese	16	100g pine nuts
7	200ml sour cream	17	1 leek
8	1kg frozen spinach	18	Celery
9	1kg onions	19	625g of mushrooms
10	1kg red onions	20	Fresh parsley

WEEK 4

(21) Fresh coriander

(22) 500g puff pastry

(23) 500g new potaoes

(24) 2 carrots

(25) 1kg frozen peas

(26) 250g halloumi

(27) 4 brioche rolls

(28) 2 little gem lettuces

(29) 1 cucumber

(30) 420g cherry tomatoes

(31) 2.5kg potatoes

(32) Packet of 3 peppers

(33) 4 avocados

(34) 1kg rice

(35) 1 courgette

(36) 326g tin of sweetcorn

(37) 1.5kg plain flour

Shopping list for lunch and dinner for 2 for 7 days

DAY-BY-DAY VEGETARIAN
MENU FOR WEEK 4

This second week of vegetarian dishes is a bit more traditional than the previous week. There's a delicious halloumi burger that's one of our regular favourites, plus a puff pastry vegetarian wellington, filled with mushrooms and spinach. There's also a torta pasquale, which is a traditional Mediterranean recipe to celebrate Easter.

Maybe you'll have a go at making your own pasta, filled with feta cheese and spinach. You can see how easy fresh pasta is to make on page 18, with my photographed step-by-step guide.

Day 1
Lunch
Jacket potato with cheese

Dinner
Spinach & feta mezzelune pasta

Day 2
Lunch
Pea soup

Dinner
Veggie wellington with new potatoes & vegetables

Day 3
Lunch
Leftover wellington with potato salad

Dinner
Halloumi burger with chips & salad

Day 4
Lunch
Egg salad rolls

Dinner
Torta pasquale & salad

Day 5
Lunch
Leftover Torta

Dinner
Mushroom stroganoff with rice & peas

Day 6
Lunch
Rice salad

Dinner
Red onion & cheese puff tart with roasted vegetables

Day 7
Lunch
Cheese sandwich

Dinner
Halloumi wraps with sweetcorn salsa

spinach & feta
MEZZELUNE PASTA

Buying fresh filled pasta in supermarkets can be expensive, so I've added this recipe to show you how easy it is to make your own, It's really just flour, water and an egg to make the plain pasta dough, which can be shaped however you like – from simple lasagna sheets and tagliatelle to more interesting filled shapes like these spinach mezzelune pockets.

Serves 2 with leftovers

Ingredients for the spinach and feta filling:

75g feta or Greek salad cheese
150g frozen spinach
1/2 small onion, finely chopped
Salt and pepper
1/2 tablespoon of oil
3-4 sage leaves, finely chopped

Ingredients for the fresh pasta:

200g plain flour
1/2 tablespoon salt
75ml water
I egg

Ingredients for the sage butter:

I lemon, grated zest only
10 fresh sage leaves, shredded, and stalks discarded
I garlic clove, crushed
50g butter
Salt and pepper
Grated cheese
Teaspoon crushed/chopped pine nuts (optional)

Firstly make up your filling by finely chopping the onion and frying for 10 minutes in oil on a medium heat.

Defrost the spinach, squeezing out the liquid before adding to the onions and cooking for about 3 minutes more to dry out. Remove and tip into a bowl, then set aside to cool down. Once cool mix with the feta cheese and salt and pepper.

Next make your pasta as per the recipe on page 18.

Roll out your pasta dough and cut out circles with a large 8cm cookie cutter. Put a small amount of the cooled spinach filling on one half of the circle, leaving room around to seal it.

With a wet finger (don't lick it, use a bowl of water), dab around the edge of the circle and close up. Seal it all the way around by gently pressing it together.

Repeat until the mixture is finished or the dough is used up. It'll make around 26-30 discs.

Before you cook the pasta, make the sage butter by putting the sage, garlic and butter into a saucepan large enough to hold all the pasta once cooked. Place over a low heat until the butter melts, then simmer gently for 5 minutes. Remove from the heat and leave to infuse.

When you have made all the mezzelune and the butter is resting, in a large pan of boiling water, cook the pasta for about 3-5 minutes, then take them out with a slotted spoon and add to the pan of sage butter. Stir gently to combine.

Season with salt and pepper then serve with a drizzle of olive oil, some crushed pine nuts and shavings of cheese.

MEAL UNDER 70p EACH

MEAL UNDER
£1.20
EACH

VEGGIE WELLINGTION
with herby new potatoes and vegetables

My husband says this isn't a wellington, it's a vegetarian giant roll. I'm calling it a wellington, and as I'm writing the recipes, I can call it whatever I like. Whatever you call it, it makes a perfect change from a nut roast for Sundays if you're giving up meat. The rest of the pastry is used for other recipes this week or you could make the apple puffs on page 190.

Serves 2 with leftovers

Ingredients for the veggie wellington:
1 tablespoon unsalted butter
1 leek, finely chopped
1 celery stalk, finely chopped
200g mushrooms, finely chopped
2 garlic cloves, crushed
200g frozen spinach, defrosted
Handful of chopped fresh parsley
2 sprigs of fresh rosemary, chopped (optional)
Handful of chopped fresh thyme
1 tablespoon crushed pine nuts
1/2 teaspoon salt and pinch of pepper
1 teaspoon Dijon mustard
200g puff pastry
1 egg

To serve:
300g new potatoes
2 carrots, peeled and chopped
200g frozen peas
Vegetarian gravy

Preheat the oven to 190°C. Then oil and flour a baking tray.

Put the defrosted spinach in a sieve and squeeze out as much water as you can.

In a large saucepan, melt the butter and cook the leeks and celery for about 10 minutes, until soft.

Add the mushrooms, and pine nuts and continue to cook for another 10 minutes. Next add the garlic and cook for a minute more then stir in the spinach.

Stir in the herbs and season with salt and pepper to taste, then set aside to cool.

On a floured surface, roll out half the puff pastry to flatten it to 5mm thick and then lay it on the prepared baking tray.

Pile the filling in an even layer in the centre of the pastry, leaving 2cm all around. Brush the exposed edges with an egg wash.

Roll out the other half of pastry and lay this over the top of the filling. Press around the edges with your fingers to seal it. Then using a fork press gently around to crimp. Brush with the egg wash, then with a sharp knife cut diagonal lines across the top and decorate with pastry leaves if you want.

Bake in the oven for 30 minutes until golden brown. Allow to cool slightly before serving. Cover with foil if it looks like it might go too dark.

Serve with boiled new potatoes with butter and chopped mint leaves, and some peas, carrots and gravy.

MEAL UNDER
£1.50
EACH

HALLOUMI BURGER
with chips and salad

Who says you can't have burger and chips if you're vegetarian? We often make this burger with halloumi instead of meat as it's so delicious. You can cook this on a barbecue or griddle pan like we did, but a lightly oiled frying pan will do the job just as well. With the red onions, lettuce and avocado, you're well on your way to your 5-a-day too.

Serves 2

Ingredients for the pickled red onions:
¹/₂ small red onion, peeled and thinly sliced
3 tablespoons white wine vinegar
1 pinch of salt

Ingredients for the avocado spread:
Squeeze of lemon
Small bunch of coriander
1 tablespoon of mayonnaise
2 avocados, mashed
Salt and pepper, to taste

Ingredients for the potato wedges:
2 medium potatoes
2 tablespoons cooking oil
Pinch of salt

Ingredients for the halloumi burger:
125g (half the packet) of halloumi, cut into 4 slices
2 brioche rolls
30g lettuce
Sweet chilli sauce or ketchup (optional)

Serve with a small mixed salad:
A few lettuce leaves
A few tomatoes chopped up
Some carrots, sliced
Some slices of cucumber

Start by pickling the red onions in a small bowl with the vinegar and salt for at least 10 minutes.

Next up make the avocado spread by mixing the mashed avocado with the mayonnaise, a squeeze of lemon juice, chopped coriander and a pinch of salt and pepper.

After these are done you can get on with the potato wedges. Firstly slice the potatoes into wedges, toss in a tray with a little oil and pinch of salt, then put in the oven for 25-30 minutes, turning them halfway through.

This would now be a good time to make the salad.

When the potatoes are nearly ready, heat up a lightly oiled griddle pan and cook the halloumi for about 2 minutes on each side, until golden brown.

Next to the halloumi lightly toast the brioche rolls on the insides for about one minute.

Layer up the burger by firstly spreading the avocado mixture on the bottom, then the lettuce, the halloumi and lastly the drained onions. Next drizzle over the chilli sauce, before putting the grilled brioche tops on.

Serve with salad and potato wedges.

Watch out as this burger is very messy to eat!

TORTA PASQUALE
& salad

This recipe is tradionally made in Italy for Easter using wild dandelions and nettles. I decided that instead I'd use frozen spinach in my version, but feel free to go foraging if you wish – I have been known to do that myself. Although this tort is made with puff pastry, short crust would work too, but my family's favourite is when we make it with filo brushed with lots of butter.

Serves 2 with leftovers

Ingredients for the torta:

Butter, for greasing the cake tin
2 tablespoons plain flour, for dusting
3 free-range eggs, plus 1 egg for wash
200g defrosted spinach
1 tablespoon oil
1 onion, finely chopped
250g cream cheese
100g feta, or Greek salad cheese
Salt and pepper
1/2 teaspoon mixed herbs
200g puff pastry

Serve with a small mixed salad:

A few lettuce leaves
A few slices of peppers, chopped up
A few tomatoes, chopped up
Some slices of cucumber
1 red onion, finely sliced

Preheat the oven to 200°C.

Place 3 eggs into a pan of boiling water and boil for about 10 minutes. Drain and place in cold water to stop them cooking any more. Once cool, remove the shells and cut in half, lengthways.

Grease a 20cm round, loose bottom cake tin with butter.

Put the defrosted spinach in a sieve and squeeze out as much of the liquid as possible.

Heat a frying pan and add the olive oil, onion and salt and pepper. Fry gently until softened, it should be about 10 minutes. Set aside and allow to cool.

Add the cooked onion to the spinach with the herbs, a little more salt and pepper, and the cheeses and mix well.

Roll out the puff pastry to 5mm and carefully line the cake tin leaving the pastry to over hang the sides, but also making sure it's tucked right into the corners. You can use a small piece of pastry to push it in. Try not to tear the pastry – if you do just patch it up. It's supposed to look a little rough, but you need to make sure it doesn't leak.

Next fill with half of the spinach and cheese mixture. Lay in the boiled egg halves, yolks down, evenly spaced, and top with the remaining spinach mixture. Then fold over the excess pastry to cover the top completely.

Brush the pastry with the egg wash and bake in the oven for 35-40 minutes, until risen and golden brown.

Remove from the oven and allow to cool before cutting.

MUSHROOM STROGANOFF
with rice & peas

The history of this stroganoff dish seems to go back to Russia in the 1870s, but there are lots of different variations from all around the world. Stroganoff can be made from beef, pork, chicken or mushrooms – like this tasty recipe here. With the paprika and English mustard, it has a delicious peppery taste set in a creamy sauce and served with rice or pasta.

Serves 2

Ingredients for the mushroom stroganoff:
1 tablespoon butter
1 tablespoon olive oil
1 onion, finely diced
2 garlic cloves, crushed
400g mushrooms, any type, cleaned and sliced
1 teaspoon English mustard
1 teaspoon paprika
250ml hot vegetable stock, made from a stock cube or homemade
200ml soured cream
$\frac{1}{2}$ lemon
Salt and black pepper
Dusting of Paprika, to finish

Ingredients for the rice and peas:
$\frac{1}{2}$ cup rice
100g frozen peas

In a deep frying pan cook the onions in the oil and butter on a medium heat for about 10 minutes or until soft.

Add the crushed garlic and continue to cook for a few minutes more.

Now add the mushrooms and cook gently for about 5-10 minutes, until the mushrooms are soft.

Add the mustard and paprika and mix well to coat everything.

Next add the stock, stirring as you pour. Simmer gently for about 5 minutes while you cook the rice.

Cook the rice according to the packet instructions in a separate saucepan until tender. At the same time cook the peas in boiling water. Season each with a little salt.

Remove the mushrooms from the heat, and stir in the soured cream with a squeeze of lemon and season to taste.

Serve the stroganoff with a dusting of paprika and the rice and peas mixed together.

MEAL UNDER
£1.40
EACH

RED ONION & CHEESE PUFF TART
with roasted vegetables

The last piece of puff pastry is saved for this delicious red onion tart. I've made this a few times and is always surprises me how tasty a scrap of pastry and a few red onions can be. It's a real leftover recipe. Finishing up the last of the courgette, peppers and mushrooms by roasting them up.

Serves 2

Ingredients for the Roasted vegetables:
1 red pepper, cut into chunks
1 green pepper, cut into chunks
1 red onion, cut into chunks
1 courgette, cut into 1cm slices
8-10 baby tomatoes
4-5 mushrooms, halved to a similar size
2 garlic cloves in skin but squashed
1 tablespoon oil
Pinch of salt and pepper
1 teaspoon dried mixed herbs

Ingredients for the filling:
1 tablespoon oil
2 medium red onions, peeled and thinly sliced
2 tablespoons white wine vinegar
1 tablespoons sugar
40g Cheddar cheese, grated
1 beaten egg for wash
Pinch of salt and pepper

Ingredients for the red onion tart:
100g puff pastry, rolled out to 3mm thick

25g feta, or Greek salad cheese to serve

Preheat the oven to 200°C.

Firstly put all the roasted vegetables except the tomatoes in a roasting tray and drizzle over the oil and seasoning. Roast for about 30 minutes, popping the tomatoes in halfway through.

To make the filling, heat the oil in a large frying pan, then fry the red onions gently for about 10 minutes, stirring occasionally, until softened.

Stir in the white wine vinegar and sugar, increasing the heat and stir frequently for another 15 minutes until the onions turn a deep caramel colour.

On a floured surface, roll out the pastry to about a 20cm x 10cm rectangle and place onto an oiled and floured baking sheet.

Sprinkle half the Cheddar cheese over the pastry, leaving a 3cm border around the edge, then spoon the caramelized onions over the cheese.

Fold the uncovered dough edges over the edge of the filling to form a rim.

Brush the rim with beaten egg or milk, and season with a little salt and pepper.

Scatter over the remaining cheese and bake for about 18-20 minutes, until golden.

Serve while hot with the roasted vegetables and some feta cheese broken over.

MEAL UNDER
£1.50
EACH

HALLOUMI WRAPS
with sweetcorn salsa

A small tin sweetcorn adds a lovely sweetness to this tomato and onion salsa and works perfectly with the mashed avocado and squeaky halloumi. You could buy wraps, but it's so easy to knock up a batch it hardly seems worth it.

Serves 2

Ingredients for the filling:
125g halloumi cheese, thickly sliced
$\frac{1}{2}$ teaspoon dried oregano
1 tablespoon olive oil
1 lemon
Small bunch of coriander, chopped
1 tablespoon mayonnaise
2 avocados, mashed
Salt and pepper, to taste

Ingredients for the wraps:
125g plain flour, plus extra for dusting
(you can use gluten free bread flour instead
with $\frac{1}{2}$ teaspoon xanthan gum)
$\frac{1}{2}$ tablespoon of oil
75ml water
$\frac{1}{2}$ teaspoon salt

Ingredients for the sweetcorn salsa:
100g tinned sweetcorn, drained
A few tomatoes, chopped finely
1 small red onion, finely chopped
$\frac{1}{2}$ bunch of coriander, chopped
Squeeze of lemon
Salt and pepper
A little olive oil

Firstly sprinkle the halloumi on both sides with pepper and oregano.

To make the wraps, sift the flour in a bowl with the salt and make a dip in the middle. Pour in the oil and mix together with a fork, then add the water and mix with your hands until you have a dough. Ideally leave it to rest for around an hour.

To make the sweetcorn salsa, mix all the ingredients together, then just before serving dress with salt and pepper, a squeeze of lemon juice and a teaspoon of oil.

Now mix the mashed avocado with the mayonnaise, a splash of lemon, chopped coriander and a pinch of salt and pepper.

On a flour-dusted surface, roll the dough into a long sausage and cut into 4 equal slices. Then roll each one into a ball.

With a rolling pin, roll each ball thinly to about 20-25cm and place on a plate with a dusting of flour between them.

In a dry frying pan cook the wraps on each side for about a minute or until cooked but not too coloured. Stack them covered in a damp towel in a low oven until needed.

Next in a large non-stick frying pan, heat the oil and quickly fry the halloumi on both sides until golden brown. Squeeze over a little lemon.

To serve, spread the avocado over the breads then divide the halloumi mixture between them and scatter over the sweetcorn salsa and roll up, ready to dive into.

MEAL UNDER
£1.50
EACH

WEEK 5

①	1 loaf sliced wholemeal bread	⑩	Garlic
②	Olive spread	⑪	Chillies
③	Salted butter	⑫	Fresh parsley
④	4 pints of milk	⑬	2 little gem lettuces
⑤	12 free-range eggs	⑭	1 cucumber
⑥	250g Cheddar cheese	⑮	Packet of 6 tomatoes
⑦	1kg onions	⑯	6 peppers
⑧	1kg red onion	⑰	Celery
⑨	1 lemon	⑱	1 x 400g tin chickpeas

19 1 × 400g tin haricot or mixed beans	**28** 1kg brown rice
20 1 × 400g tin tomatoes	**29** 2.5kg potatoes
21 Packet of radishes	**30** 227g tin pineapple
22 Bunch of spring onions	**31** 1.5kg plain flour
23 1kg sweet potaoes	**32** 200g natural yogurt
24 1 whole free-range chicken	**33** 1kg frozen peas
25 550g frozen basa white fish fillets	
26 380g turkey steaks	
27 200g chorizo	Shopping list for lunch and dinner for 2 for 7 days

DAY-BY-DAY HEALTHIER CARBS
MENU FOR WEEK 5

Week 5 is designed as a lower carbohydrate week, so no refined white pasta, bread and rice. Instead I've added some sweet potatoes and brown rice. It isn't strictly low carb, it's just a bit lower. It's more about swapping in a few healthier alternatives.

If you're leaving out some carbohydrates you'll need to add more protein in the form of meat, fish and pulses to keep you feeling fuller for longer. There's also plenty of vegetables and salad to help bulk out the meals and give you a proper balanced diet. Just because you're eating healthy doesn't mean you can't still have delicious meals.

Day 1
Lunch
Cheese sandwich

Dinner
Mediterranean fish bake

Day 2
Lunch
Pea soup

Dinner
Piri-Piri chicken with loaded sweet potato & salad

Day 3
Lunch
Egg Salad

Dinner
Sweet & sour turkey on brown rice

Day 4
Lunch
Brown rice salad

Dinner
Chicken & chorizo traybake with roasted sweet potato and vegetables

Day 5
Lunch
Leftover roasted veg and rice salad (see page 21)

Dinner
Turkey schnitzels with sweet potato wedges & salad

Day 6
Lunch
Egg salad sandwich

Dinner
Gumbo with brown rice

Day 7
Lunch
Rice salad

Dinner
Chorizo & bean stew with yogurt bread roti

Mediterranean
FISH BAKE

This fish dish is adapted from one we have quite regularly at home as we always have a bit of frozen fish in the freezer that needs using up. I'm forever buying fish when I see it on special offer as it's so versatile for curries and rice dishes. Because the potato is so thinly cut, you get lots of lovely crispy edges that curl up when it's baked in the oven. Delicious.

Serves 2

Ingredients for the fish bake:
4 white fish fillets, defrosted
1 red pepper, thinly sliced
1 yellow pepper, thinly sliced
1 medium onion, thinly sliced
3-4 tomatoes, thinly sliced
Handful of chopped parsley
1/4 teaspoon chilli flakes or finely chopped chilli
1 teaspoon paprika
2 tablespoons olive oil
200g potato, thinly sliced

Firstly carefully cut all the vegetables into very thin slices with a mandolin or knife.

Preheat your oven to 190°C.

Gently fry the onions on a low heat for about 10-15 minutes until soft with a tablespoon of oil.

While these are cooking parboil the sliced potato for about 3 minutes in salted water and drain.

Spread half the onions, peppers and tomatoes in the bottom of an ovenproof dish, then layer half the potatoes.

Next cut the fish into 2cm chunks and lay this on top, then scatter the parsley, chilli flakes and salt and pepper.

Layer the other half of the onions, peppers and tomatoes, and finish with the rest of the potato, which should cover the dish.

Drizzle over the rest of the olive oil and salt and pepper. Then cover with foil and bake in the oven for about 20-25 minutes.

Remove the foil about half way through to crisp up the potato.

Serve with a scatter of chopped parsley.

MEAL UNDER
£2.70
EACH

PERI-PERI CHICKEN
with loaded sweet potato and salad

So, my confession here is that I've only been to Nando's once, mainly because I wanted to see what all the fuss was about. I had to test this dish on a few of my friends that love the place to see if it was as good as their Portuguese piri-piri sauce. Well they all asked for the recipe, so it must have passed the test.

Serves 2

Ingredients for the piri-piri sauce:
4-6 fresh red chillies, depending on how hot you want it
3-4 garlic cloves crushed
$1/2$ teaspoon salt
$1/2$ teaspoon oregano
$1/2$ teaspoon paprika
3 tablespoons of oil
3 tablespoons of red wine vinegar
$1/2$ juice of a lemon
Dash of Worcestershire sauce

Ingredients for the piri-piri chicken:
2 free-range chicken breasts save the little inside fillets bits for the gumbo later in the week
Salt and freshly ground black pepper

Ingredients for the loaded sweet potatoes:
2 sweet jacket potato
1 spring onion finely slices
100g of cheese
Salt and pepper
$1/4$ teaspoon of Dijon mustard

Serve with a small mixed salad:
A few lettuce leaves
A few peppers, chopped up
A few tomatoes, chopped up
Some slices of cucumber
1 spring onion, finely sliced
A few radishes, quartered

To make the piri-piri sauce prick and roast the chillies in the oven for about 10 minutes.

Chop the chillies, and place them in a saucepan along with the garlic, salt, oregano, paprika, olive oil and vinegar and simmer for about 5 minutes to thicken slightly.

Blend it into a purée with a hand blender or food processor. Place the chicken breast in a clean freezer bag and add half the piri-piri sauce, spreading it evenly over the chicken.

Seal the bag and marinate in the refrigerator for at least an hour. Save the rest in a small bowl for brushing on later.

preheat the oven to 180°C.

Pop 2 sweet potatoes in the microwave for 6-8 minutes to start them, then bake in the oven until soft.

Meanwhile season the marinated chicken, and cook on a griddle or frying pan for 2-3 minutes on each side, until golden brown.

Transfer the griddled chicken to a roasting tray and brush over some more piri-piri sauce, then roast in the oven for 20-25 minutes, until cooked through, basting regularly with the remaining piri-piri sauce.

To make the loaded sweet potatoes, slice in half and scoop out the potato. Mash and mix with the salt and pepper, onion, half the cheese and the mustard and refill the skins. Sprinkle the remaining cheese over the top and grill for a few minutes until the cheese is golden.

Serve the chicken with the loaded sweet potato and salad.

SWEET & SOUR TURKEY
on brown rice

Although brown rice is still a carb, it's a whole grain that contains the bran and germ. These provide fibre and several vitamins and minerals, unlike white rice that, has had them stripped out. As long as you don't have too much, a $1/4$ cup each before cooking is fine as part of a balanced diet. So if you're craving a Chinese takeaway hopefully this homemade sweet and sour meal will keep you on the straight and narrow.

Serves 2

Ingredients for the sweet & sour turkey:

250ml chicken stock
2 tablespoons soy sauce
2 tablespoons cornstarch
2 tablespoons butter
1 onion, diced
$1/2$ red pepper, diced
$1/2$ green pepper, diced
$1/2$ teaspoon ground ginger
$1/2$ teaspoon salt
$1/4$ teaspoon pepper
200g tin pineapple chunks with juice
1 dessertspoon cider vinegar
1 tablespoon sugar
190g ($1/2$ packet) turkey, diced

1 cup of brown rice, save half for rice salad

Firstly start the rice cooking according to the packet instructions.

Brown rice will take a little longer than white so you'll need to factor this in.

Next mix together 100ml of the chicken stock, soy sauce and cornstarch in a bowl.

Heat the butter in a large saucepan, add the onion, diced turkey, bell pepper, ginger, salt and pepper.

Stir to coat with the butter, cover and cook, stirring occasionally, for about 10 minutes.

Add the pineapple, the remaining 150ml of chicken stock, vinegar and sugar to the saucepan and stir to mix well.

Pour in the cornstarch mixture and turn up the heat.

Once the mixture begins to simmer, turn the heat to low and cook uncovered for 10 minutes.

Serve with a little chopped parsley for colour if you have it.

MEAL UNDER
£1.50
EACH

CHICKEN & CHORIZO TRAYBAKE
with roasted sweet potato and vegetables

We often make this kind of dish when we get home from work, as it's so simple. You just chop and chuck everything in a roasting tray, add some herbs and spices then pop it in the oven and leave it for 45 minutes while you pour yourself a glass of wine and watch your favourite soap opera.

Serves 2

Ingredients for the traybake:
1 medium sweet potato, unpeeled but washed and cut into 2cm cubes
2 large ripe tomatoes, cut into 4 wedges
1 large red onion, cut into 8 wedges
1/2 red pepper, cut into large chunks
1/2 yellow pepper, cut into large chunks
2 free-range chicken thighs, skin on
90g chorizo sausage thickly sliced
4 garlic cloves
1 teaspoon paprika
2 tablespoons cooking oil
2 tablespoons balsamic vinegar
1/2 teaspoon thyme
Pinch of salt and pepper

Preheat the oven to 180°C.

Quarter the tomatoes and cut up the sweet potato, then place them in a large roasting tray.

Peel the onion and cut into large wedges, then de-seed and roughly chop the peppers. Cut the sausage in to 1 cm slices and add all these to the tray along with the chicken thighs.

Gently squash but leave whole the unpeeled garlic cloves with the side of your knife and add to the tray with the paprika.

Add the oil, balsamic vinegar, herbs and a good pinch of salt and pepper.

Toss everything together with your hands, placing the chicken skin side up on top of the vegetables.

Roast for around 45 minutes, or until the chicken is golden and cooked through, and the potatoes are soft. Turn the vegetables and chorizo half way through, but leave the chicken on top to crisp the skin.

Serve with some cooked peas or green veg.

Save back a little of the roasted vegetables for lunch.

TURKEY SCHNITZELS
with sweet potato wedges and salad

If you're on a lower carb diet, one way to still get your chip fix is to swap to sweet potatoes instead. Although they still contain similar carbs to a normal spud, they count as a very good one of your 5-a-day. Using lean turkey steaks instead of pork in the schnitzel is a great source of protein, which is another important part of a balanced diet.

Serves 2

Ingredients for the turkey schnitzels:
190g (½ packet) turkey steaks
Pinch of salt and pepper
3 tablespoons plain flour
1 crust of bread, made in to fine bread crumbs
1 egg, beaten

Ingredients for the wedges:
2 sweet potatoes
2 tablespoons cooking oil
Pinch of salt
A few stalks of rosemary, leaves picked and roughly chopped

Serve with a small mixed salad:
A few lettuce leaves
A few slices of pepper, chopped up
A few tomatoes, chopped up
Some slices of cucumber

Preheat your oven to 200°C.

In 3 separate bowls put flour, the beaten egg with salt and pepper, and some bread crumbs.

Firstly dip the turkey steaks in the flour, then the egg and lastly the bread crumbs.

Pour some oil in a shallow pan and fry the turkey steaks for a few minutes either side, until the crumb goes a golden brown.

Then lay them on a baking tray and finish off in the oven for about 10 minutes until cooked through.

For the wedges, cut the potatoes lengthways into wedges – you should get about 6-8 per potato.

Drizzle over the oil and salt, then with your hands give it a good mix coating the potatoes all over.

Put in the oven and cook for 15 minutes.

Take the leaves off the rosemary and roughly chop them.

After the 15 minutes is up, take the wedges out of the oven and give them a turning and mixing again to brown the other side, then scatter the rosemary over them.

Cook for another 10-15 minutes until golden and crunchy on the outside and soft and fluffy in the middle.

Serve with a mixed salad and mayonnaise to dip in.

UNDER
£1.50
EACH

GUMBO
with brown rice

I've eaten gumbo a few times, even in Americas Deep South where it comes from, and have always been a bit disappointed. A lot of people rave about it so I thought maybe I just wasn't getting it right. As gumbo is a cheap recipe I really wanted to master it, and this time I have. I made it as I normally would but added 2 teaspoons of Worcestershire sauce to balance out the pepper and it really works.

Serves 2

Ingredients for the gumbo:

4 tablespoons of oil
2 free-range drumsticks, skin on, plus small fillets
1 onion, chopped
2 celery sticks, sliced
3 bay leaves
50g chorizo, cut into chunks
3 tablespoons plain flour
1 teaspoon paprika
1 teaspoon ground cumin
1 teaspoon ground chilli
1 teaspoon dried mixed herbs
600ml strong chicken stock, using 1 stock cube
1 yellow pepper, de-seeded and cut into chunks
2 teaspoons Worcestershire sauce
1 spring onion, sliced
Handful of roughly chopped parsley

Serve with $1/2$ cup of brown rice

Added options ingredients:

You can use a couple of sausages, chopped up, instead of the chorizo

Heat 1 tablespoon of oil in a deep saucepan and fry the chicken for about 15 minutes to brown.

Take out and put on a plate, then add the onions to the pan with another tablespoon of oil, and fry for 5 minutes until almost softened.

Now add the celery and the bay leaves and keep frying for another few minutes, then tip out to join the chicken.

Add the last 2 tablespoons of oil and flour to this pan and cook it into a kind of paste.

Cook, for a minute stirring constantly, then stir in the spices for another minute, before gradually adding the stock, stirring until the sauce is smooth. Use a balloon whisk or fork if you need to.

Return the chicken and vegetables to the pan, with the chopped peppers and chorizo and cover with a lid. Simmer gently for about 15 minutes, stirring every now and then to stop it sticking to the bottom of the pan.

While this is simmering, cook the rice according to the packet instructions. Brown rice will take a little longer than white so you'll need to factor this in.

Season to taste and serve the gumbo in a bowl with the rice and the spring onions, and chopped parsley on top.

CHORIZO & BEAN STEW
with yogurt bread roti

There's plenty of fibre and protein in these beans, which if you're on a low carb diet will keep you fuller for longer, so you won't be tempted to snack on sweet treats. The easy homemade flatbreads are ideal for mopping up the delicious paprika flavours from this healthy stew.

Serves 2

Ingredients for the roti flatbreads:
125g plain flour, plus extra for dusting
$1/2$ teaspoon baking powder
125g natural yoghurt

Ingredients for the chorizo & bean stew:
3 tablespoons of olive oil
1 onion, chopped
3 cloves garlic, crushed
60g chorizo sausage, diced
$1/2$ green pepper, sliced
$1/2$ red pepper, sliced
2 bay leaves
100ml red wine or 3 tablespoons of balsamic vinegar
1 teaspoon paprika
400g tin chopped tomatoes
400g tin chickpeas, drained
400g tin haricot or mixed beans, drained
Salt and pepper to taste
Little chopped parsley for topping

Firstly make the flatbread dough as this can be set aside while you cook the stew.

To make the roti flatbread, mix all the ingredients together in a bowl. Then on a clean flour dusted surface knead for a few minutes.

This can now wait in a the bowl until you're ready to cook the breads.

Fry the onion and garlic for a few minutes until starting to soften. Add the diced chorizo, peppers, and bay leaves and cook for a few more minutes.

Add the red wine or balsamic vinegar, paprika, and chopped tomatoes. Give it all a mix together.

Simmer for about 5-7 minutes, until the sauce reduces slightly.

Add the washed and drained chickpeas and beans, cover the pan and cook for another 5 minutes on a low heat to warm through. Season to taste.

Divide the dough into 4 balls and roll out each one until about 3mm thick.

Heat up a frying pan, and dry fry for a few minutes on each side until the little pockets of air turn the bread golden, as the photo shows.

Serve with the flatbread and a sprinkle of fresh parsley.

WEEK 6

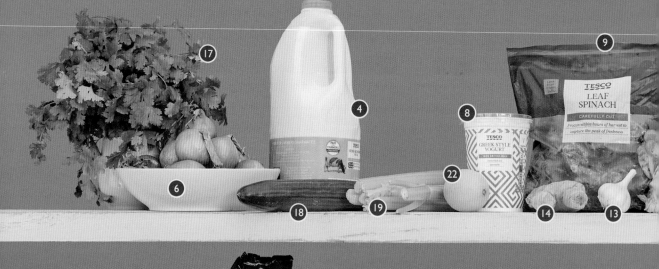

1	1 loaf sliced wholemeal bread		12	250g feta/Greek
2	Olive spread		13	Garlic
3	Salted butter		14	Ginger
4	4 pints of milk		15	Chillies
5	12 free-range eggs		16	Fresh parsley
6	1kg onions		17	Fresh coriander
7	1kg red onions		18	1 cucumber
8	500g natural yogurt		19	Celery
9	1kg frozen spinach		20	Packet of 3 peppers
10	200g cashews		21	2 little gem lettuces
11	270g filo pastry		22	1 lemon

23	2 carrots	34	1 large cauliflower
24	Packet of 6 tomatoes	35	1 large sweet potato
25	Bunch of spring onions	36	500g coucous
26	153g jar pitted olives	37	1.5g plain flour
27	1 large butternut squash	38	340g crunchy peanut butter
28	1 x 400g tin tomatoes	39	1 lime
29	500g risotto rice	40	250g noodles
30	480g jar roasted peppers	41	300g bean sprouts
31	250g ricotta		
32	125g mozzarella		
33	250g Cheddar cheese		Shopping list for lunch and dinner for 2 for 7 days

DAY-BY-DAY HEALTHIER CARBS VEGETARIAN
MENU FOR WEEK 6

This week's menu has plenty of vegetables and salad to give you a balanced diet, but adding the peanut butter and dairy should help you keep the hunger at bay. Instead of pasta this week I've used a butternut squash to make a delicious rotolo and noodles for a tasty pad thai that's full of flavour.

If you're leaving out more carbohydrates and meats you'll have to really think carefully about how to get more protein in your diet to help you stay fuller for longer. So more beans and pulses would be good as well as the free-range eggs at lunch times.

Day 1
Lunch
Scrambled egg on toast

Dinner
Spinach & feta sigara börek with Greek salad

Day 2
Lunch
Onion soup, (see page 34)

Dinner
Spinach & ricotta rotolo butternut squash

Day 3
Lunch
Egg salad

Dinner
Caribbean vegetable traybake on couscous salad

Day 4
Lunch
Couscous salad

Dinner
Cauliflower cheese with a crunchy topping

Day 5
Lunch
Cheese salad sandwich

Dinner
Vegetable samosas with spicy salad & mint yogurt dip

Day 6
Lunch
Leftover cauliflower cheese

Dinner
Roasted butternut squash risotto

Day 7
Lunch
Risotto leftovers

Dinner
Vegetable pad thai in peanut sauce

SPINACH & FETA SIGARA BÖREK
with Greek salad & Tzatziki

As Turkey and Greece being are close in the Mediterranean, a lot of their dishes are very similar. This recipe is one of the first I learnt in an evening cookery class a few years ago but now by baking these it is a much healthier option than frying them.

Serves 2

Ingredients for the Börek:
1 tablespoon oil, for frying
1 onion, finely chopped
100g frozen spinach
2 garlic cloves, crushed
150g feta or Greek salad cheese
Salt and pepper
Small sprigs of parsley leaves, chopped (optional)
1/4 teaspoon salt and a pinch of pepper
1 tablespoon oil, for baking
125g (half a packet) filo pastry (125g)

Ingredients for the tzatziki:
3 tablespoons Greek or natural yogurt
1/4 cucumber, grated
2 garlic cloves, crushed
1/4 tablespoon olive oil
Few drops of lemon juice
Handful of fresh mint leaves from the garden, finely chopped, or use mint sauce and less lemon
Pinch of salt and pepper

Ingredients for the Greek-style salad:
1 small red onion, finely sliced
3 inches of cucumber, sliced
2 tomatoes, cut into chunks
Handful of olives
50g of the feta, or Greek salad cheese, broken over
Drizzle of olive oil
Salt and pepper

Thaw the spinach and put it into a sieve over the sink, press down hard to squeeze out as much water as you can.

Preheat the oven: 200°C

Cook the onions and garlic on a medium heat in the oil for about 8-10 minutes, then add them to the spinach, and the crumbled feta cheese and mix very well. Add the salt and pepper.

Cut the filo sheets in half and put the rest back in the box in the fridge. The filo you're using mustn't dry out so keep it under a damp tea towel while you work.

Place one half sheet of filo pastry on the work surface. Brush it with oil, then place another sheet on top.

Place one heaped tablespoon of the filling on the lower side of each rectangle. Fold the sides over the filling and roll the pastry into the shape shown in the photo.

Place the rolls on an oiled baking sheet with the seam facing down and brush with oil.

Bake for about 20 minutes or until golden brown. Cover the rolls loosely with aluminium foil after half the time if they seem to get too dark.

To make the tzatziki, cut the cucumber in half and scoop out and discard the seeds. Grate the cucumber, pat the excess water off with a paper towel and mix into the yogurt and other ingredients. Season to taste.

Serve with tzatziki and Greek salad.

MEAL UNDER
£1.90
EACH

SPINACH & RICOTTA
rotolo butternut squash

If you're trying to eat a lower carb diet, this dish could be perfect for you. Instead of cannelloni pasta, I've used butternut squash. It may not look as uniform but I love the twisting and turning of the thin slices that will be covered in the melted cheese and spinach mixture.

Serves 2

Ingredients for the rotolo:
1/4 large butternut squash, cut into thin strips
400g tin chopped tomatoes
1 tablespoon tomato purée
2-3 garlic cloves, crushed
1 onion finely, chopped
2 roasted peppers from the jar, chopped
1/2 teaspoon mixed herbs
250g ricotta
125g frozen spinach, defrosted and chopped
125g mozzarella
50g Cheddar cheese, grated
Salt and black pepper

Serve with a small mixed salad:
A few lettuce leaves
A few slices of peppers, chopped up
A few tomatoes, chopped up
Some slices of cucumber
1 red onion, finely sliced

Preheat the oven to 180°C

Cook the onion, stirring, for about 10 minutes or until softened. Add the garlic, then cook for another few minutes.

Transfer half the onion mixture to a small saucepan. Stir in the tomatoes, roasted peppers and tomato purée. Season with salt and pepper, then simmer for about 10 minutes until it thickens. Set aside.

Defrost the spinach and put it into a sieve over the sink, press down hard to squeeze out as much water as you can.

In a bowl, combine the ricotta with the cooked onion, and garlic mixture, along with the spinach, half the Cheddar, and half the mozzarella, and a big pinch of salt and pepper. Stir well to combine.

In the bottom of an ovenproof 8 inch baking dish, spread a layer of the tomato paste sauce.

Peel the butternut squash, then with a peeler or mandolin make ribbons with the butternut flesh. Roll and swirl them and place end up on the dish. Fill the middles and any holes with the ricotta mixture, repeating until you have used up the ingredients.

Top with the remaining Cheddar and the mozzarella, Cover with foil and bake for 25-30 minutes. Remove the foil and bake for a further 15 minutes or until the cheese is golden. You can grill it for the last few minutes if you can't wait.

Serve with a salad.

CARIBBEAN VEGETABLE TRAYBAKE
on couscous salad

Roasting your vegetables is a simple mid week meal, as you can just shove them in the oven and forget about them for an hour while you relax after a hard day. To save a bit of oven time later in the week you could precook half the butternut squash for the risotto recipe and store in the fridge until needed.

Serves 2 with leftovres

Ingredients for the Caribbean marinade:
2 spring onions
1/2 teaspoon dried thyme
2 fresh bay leaves
1/2 teaspoon ground cloves
1/2 teaspoon ground allspice
1/2 teaspoon ground nutmeg
3 tablespoons white wine vinegar
1 tablespoon runny honey
1-2 chillies
3 garlic cloves
3 tablespoons rum (optional)
1 tablespoon of olive oil

Ingredients for the vegetable traybake:
1/2 cauliflower head, chopped into florets
1 sweet potato, cut into 3cm cubes
1/2 red pepper, roughly chopped
1/2 green pepper, roughly chopped
1 red onion, roughly chopped
1/4 large butternut squash, cut into 3cm cubes
Pinch of salt and pepper
2 tablespoons oil

Ingredients for the couscous salad:
2 spring onions, finely chopped
1 tomato, de-seeded and finely chopped
4cm cucumber, finely chopped
100g couscous
Pinch of salt

Added options ingredients:
You can use swede, parsnip, carrot, any root vegetable that needs using up really

First make your Caribbean marinade by popping the ingredients in a blender and whizzing together. This can be made a few days before and kept in a clean jam jar in the fridge.

Preheat the oven to 190°C.

To make the traybake, chop the unpeeled sweet potato and butternut squash into 3cm chunks, cut the cauliflower into the same size and chop the red onion into large chunks.

In a medium roasting tray, mix the vegetables together with the salt, pepper and oil. Then spoon over 3 tablespoons of the marinade and with clean hands rub this into the vegetables. Roast for about 50-60 minutes, or until everything is golden and cooked through. Turn the vegetables halfway through and add the peppers, making sure they get covered in the marinade too.

While this is cooking put the leftover marinade into a small saucepan and simmer until it thickens a little. This can be poured over when you serve.

Next make the couscous salad by tipping into a large bowl the dried coucous with a pinch of salt, then fill with boiling water to 1cm above the dried couscous. Put a lid over and wait about 5-7 minutes until all the water has been sucked up.

Finely chop the salad ingredients while the couscous is cooking and tip them on top, then use a fork to break up the grains and mix them through. Season to taste.

To serve, spread the couscous over the bottom of a serving dish and spoon over of the cooked Caribbean vegetables. Save a couple of the root vegetables back for the samosas. Pour over the marinade and scatter a little parsley if you have it.

CAULIFLOWER CHEESE
with a crunchy topping

Making a white sauce for the cauliflower cheese is a great skill to master and could save you pounds not having to buy jars for lasagne, etc. I used to worry about it going lumpy but if you just keep stirring it's really easy to do. I added a cheesy bread crumb topping that takes it to the next level.

Serves 2 with leftovers

Ingredients for the cauliflower cheese:
1/2 cauliflower head, including the best leaves
20g unsalted butter
20g plain flour
300ml milk
1/2 teaspoon Dijon mustard
75g Cheddar cheese, grated

50g homemade bread crumbs
25g Cheddar cheese grated
1 tablespoon oil
Salt and pepper

Preheat the oven to 180°C.

Mix the bread crumbs with 25g of grated cheese, salt and pepper, then the oil and stir well.

You can make the bread crumbs either in a food processor or grate the crust of bread with a cheese grater. I keep the unwanted crusts and bread crumbs in the freezer for when I need them.

Now parboil the cauliflower for 5 minutes, then drain. This will save oven cooking time.

Next put a pan on a medium heat with the butter to melt.

When the butter has melted, stir in the flour for a minute to make a paste, then gradually add the milk, whisking as you go, until lovely and smooth. Make sure you keep stirring so it doesn't burn on the bottom.

When the sauce has started to thicken, add 75g of the Cheddar, the mustard and season to taste.

Arrange the florets of cauliflower in a baking dish and pour over the cheese sauce.

Scatter over the bread crumb mixture.

Bake for 30-35 minutes, or until golden and cooked through.

MEAL UNDER
60p
EACH

MEAL UNDER
£1.15
EACH

VEGETABLE SAMOSAS
with spicy salad & mint yogurt dip

I love samosas and living in west London means we have some of the best shops that sell them, but I would never have thought to make them myself before starting my budget food blog. It's a little fiddly when you first try the folding, but really it's just like origami in pastry. Maybe practise with a piece of paper first if you're unsure.

Serves 2

Ingredients for the samosas:
2 tablespoons vegetable oil
$^1/_2$ teaspoon mustard seeds
$^1/_2$ red onion, chopped
$^1/_2$ teaspoon ginger, finely chopped
40g frozen peas (optional)
1 tablespoon ground coriander
2 teaspoons ground cumin
$^1/_2$ teaspoon red chilli powder
2 teaspoons garam masala
Juice of $^1/_2$ a lemon
Pinch of salt
Splash of water
100g leftover root vegetables from the Caribbean tray bake (see page 137), diced small or 100g of boiled potatoes
$^1/_2$ a small bunch coriander stalks finely chopped
145g ($^1/_2$ packet) ready-made filo pastry, 125g
4 tablespoons melted butter, for brushing
1 tablespoon sesame seeds (optional)

Ingredients for the Asian-inspired salad:
1 teaspoon black mustard seeds
1 tablespoon oil until just starting to pop
2 large carrots, peeled and grated
100g or 1 roasted red pepper from the jar, sliced
1 small red onion, finely sliced
Handful of coriander leaves, chopped
Juice of $^1/_2$ a lemon
Salt and pepper, to taste

Cheat's mint yogurt dip:
1 teaspoon mint sauce mixed with
3 tablespoons natural yogurt

Heat the oil in a small non-stick pan and fry the mustard seeds for about 10 seconds, until they splutter. Then add the onion, coriander stalks and ginger and cook for 2-3 minutes over a high heat. Add the peas, stir well and add the spices, salt and the lemon juice.

Cook for 1-2 minutes, then add the cooked potatoes or leftover root vegetables and cook for 2-3 minutes. Taste and adjust the seasoning. Then preheat the oven to 190°C

Unroll the pastry and cover with a damp tea towel. Take one piece and keep the rest covered so that it doesn't dry out.

Lay the pastry sheet flat on a clean surface and brush with melted butter. Fold in one third of the pastry lengthways towards the middle. Brush again with the butter and fold in the other side to make a long triple-layered strip.

Place one rounded teaspoon of the filling mixture at one end of the strip, leaving a 2cm border.

Take the right corner and fold diagonally to the left, enclosing the filling and forming a triangle. Fold again along the upper crease of the triangle. Keep folding in this way until you reach the end of the strip and the filling is enclosed.

Brush the outer surface with more butter. Place onto an oiled baking sheet and cover while you make the rest of the samosas. Sprinkle over a few sesame seeds, if using.

Bake in the centre of the oven for 10-12 minutes, or until golden and crisp, turning halfway through the cooking time.

To make the salad, mix all the ingredients together and serve with the cheat's mint yogurt dip.

Roasted butternut squash
RISOTTO

I know rice isn't particularly low carb, but Arborio rice is a better source of fibre than normal white rice, and this risotto recipe contains lots of healthy vegetables, including the butternut squash. Plus this recipe is delicious and gives me the chance to photograph it in my new risotto bowls bought from a second-hand shop in Amsterdam.

Serves 2 plus leftovers

Ingredients for the risotto:
1/2 litre of fresh, hot stock, plus extra hot water if needed
150ml white wine (optional)
1 tablespoon extra virgin olive oil
1 small onion, peeled and cut into small cubes
1 stick celery, finely cut
1 carrots, peeled and cut into small cubes
125g Arborio risotto rice
Knob of butter
50g freshly grated cheese
Salt and pepper, to taste

1/4 large butternut squash, pre-cooked
Bunch of fresh sage, leaves picked (optional)

Firstly heat your stock, either by boiling a kettle for the stock cube or boiling your homemade stock in a pan.

Then fry your chopped onions, carrots and celery gently for 15 minutes. Add the rice and turn up the heat to cook for a minute stirring so as not to burn it.

Add the wine if using and cook for about 1 minute, then turn down and start adding the stock a ladleful at a time and stir. You are looking for each ladleful of stock to be absorbed before adding the next. Don't be tempted to stir the rice too much – you want the grains to cook but not break up.

The rice should take around 15 minutes to cook, with regular additions of stock and a little stir. The grains should still have a little bite to them and the dish itself will have become naturally creamy.

While this is cooking, scoop out the flesh from the skin of the pre-roasted butternut and add this to the half cooked risotto.

When the rice is cooked and creamy turn off the heat, add the cheese and let it rest for a couple of minutes with a lid on. Meanwhile, gently fry the picked sage leaves in a little hot oil.

Serve in bowls and scatter the sage

MEAL UNDER
60p
EACH

VEGETABLE PAD THAI
in peanut sauce

I'm sure we've all cooked a stir fry using those leftover bits of veg from the fridge and a sachet of bright coloured gloop from the supermarket. Well this traditional pad thai recipe takes that to the next stage. You can still use up those leftover vegetables from the fridge, but with this delicious peanut sauce you'll want this time and time again.

Serves 2

Ingredients for the sauce:
150ml vegetable stock (1/2 a vegetable stock cube, if not using homemade)
1 tablespoon soy sauce
1/2 tablespoon fish sauce
1 tablespoon brown sugar
1 tablespoon peanut butter
2 tablespoons lime juice
1 tablespoon white wine vinegar
1 chilli, thinly sliced
1/2 teaspoon ground ginger
1 clove garlic, crushed

Ingredients for the pad Thai:
125g (2 nests) egg noodles
1 teaspoon vegetable oil
1 large egg, beaten
200g (1/2 packet) bean sprouts
1/2 red pepper, finely sliced
1/2 green pepper, finely sliced
1/2 yellow pepper, finely sliced

Ingredients for the garnish:
Cashews or peanuts, chopped
Sliced chilli
A few raw bean sprouts
Lime wedges
Fresh coriander, chopped

Mix together the sauce ingredients, microwave for a few seconds to soften the peanut butter if you need to, and set aside.

Cook the noodles according to the packet instructions.

Heat a deep frying pan or wok with the oil and cook the peppers for a few minutes until just soft.

Push the peppers to the edge of the pan and pour the beaten egg in and scramble. Now add the noodles and sauce, and turn down the heat.

Cook for about 4-5 minutes stirring regularly.

Once the sauce has thickened stir in the bean sprouts to warm through, for about a minute.

Squeeze over the lime juice and serve immediately with the chopped coriander, chilli, bean sprouts and nuts.

Serve with a wedge of lime.

MEAL UNDER
£1
EACH

1	2 loaves of sliced gluten-free bread	**11**	1 cucumber
2	Olive spread	**12**	420g cherry tomatoess
3	Salted butter	**13**	Chillies
4	4 pints of milk	**14**	Packet of 3 peppers
5	12 free-range eggs	**15**	Celery
6	1kg onions	**16**	2.5kg potatoes
7	1kg red onions	**17**	1 whole free-range chicken
8	1 lemon	**18**	500g lean mince
9	1 lime	**19**	550g frozen basa white fish fillets
10	2 little gem lettuces	**20**	500g Cheddar cheese

WEEK 7

21	Garlic	**31**	Fresh sage leaves
22	2 × 400g tins of tomatoes	**32**	Fresh coriander
23	1 × 400g tin kidney beans	**33**	100g mango chutney
24	500g carots	**34**	1kg rice
25	1 × 153g jar pitted olives	**35**	1 litre sparkling water
26	1kg gluten-free flour	**36**	Ginger
27	1kg buckwheat flour		
28	100g Xanthan gum		
29	1kg fozen peas		
30	1 savoy cabbage		Shopping list for lunch and dinner for 2 for 7 days

DAY-BY-DAY GLUTEN FREE
MENU FOR WEEK 7

This week is for anyone on a gluten-free diet, whether it's through choice or you're celiac, I hope you find some recipes that you enjoy and help you save money too. I've added a couple of Gluten free loaves to the shopping budget for lunches,

For dinner there's gluten-free Yorkshire puddings, battered fish and chips and fresh pasta lasagna, as well as lots of other favourite meals that have been adapted for a gluten-free diet. Plus check out the gluten-free recipes in the Cakes and Desserts section.

Day 1
Lunch
Cheese on GF toast

Dinner
GF Breaded fish goujons with loaded skins and salad

Day 2
Lunch
Pea soup

Dinner
Chicken cacciatore with roast potatoes & GF Yorkshire pudding

Day 3
Lunch
Egg salad GF sandwich

Dinner
Pizzoccheri with cabbage & potato

Day 4
Lunch
Leftover pasta, chopped up, with salad

Dinner
Coronation chicken with curry rice

Day 5
Lunch
Leftover curry rice

Dinner
GF beef lasagne with salad

Day 6
Lunch
Leftover lasagna

Dinner
Beef & bean enchiladas with tomato salsa

Day 7
Lunch
Egg Salad

Dinner
Fried fish in gluten-free batter with paprika chips & margarita salsa

GF BREADED FISH GOUJONS
with loaded skins & salad

These fish goujons are made with crusts from the shop-brought gluten-free bread, which can be a little dry so make great bread crumbs for the fish. With the cheesy loaded potatoes and homemade tartare sauce, you won't feel like you're missing out by eating gluten free this week.

Serves 2

Ingredients for the loaded potato skins:
2 medium potatoes
50g grated cheese
$^1/_2$ small onion, finely chopped
$^1/_4$ teaspoon Dijon or wholegrain mustard

Ingredients for the fish goujons:
2 fish fillets, cut into 3cm pieces
$^1/_2$ teaspoon cayenne pepper
I egg
2 slices of GF bread crusts, blitzed into breadcrumbs
I tablespoon GF flour
Pinch of salt and pepper
Olive oil

Serve with a salad:
I baby gem lettuce, cut into chunks,
4cm of cucumber, sliced and cut into chunks
I carrot, thinly sliced with a peeler
A handful of tomatoes, cut into chunks

Ingredients for the tartare sauce:
100ml mayonnaise
2 tablespoons capers, drained and finely chopped
I tablespoon vinegar, from the capers jar
2 tablespoons gherkins, drained and finely chopped
$^1/_2$ small onion, finely chopped
Squeeze of lemon juice
2 tablespoons chopped fresh parsley or I dried
Salt and pepper

Preheat the oven to 190°C.

Firstly bake 2 potatoes for about 45 minutes until soft inside, but crunchy on the outside.

For the fish bites, firstly in a bowl mix the cayenne pepper with the gluten free flour and pinch of salt and pepper, then transfer to a clean freezer bag. Add the fish pieces and shake gently until the fish is coated.

In a food processor blitz the gluten-free bread, then add a good lug of olive oil until you have fine bread crumbs.

In one bowl beat an egg with a touch of water, in another bowl add the bread crumb mixture.

Firstly one by one dip the coated fish pieces in the egg mixture, then in the bread crumbs and place on an oiled baking tray. Pat the crumb mixture on to the fish if it's not sticking.

Cook in the oven for about 15 minutes until cooked through.

To make the loaded potatoes, slice in half and scoop out the potato. Mash and mix with the salt and pepper, onion, half the cheese and the mustard and refill the skins. Sprinkle the remaining cheese over the top and pop back in the oven for about 10 minutes until the cheese is melted and golden.

When the fish is cooked, serve with the loaded potato skins and the fresh salad.

To make the tartare sauce, mix together all of the ingredients in a small bowl and serve straight away. Taste it and adjust.

MEAL UNDER
£1.50
EACH

CHICKEN CACCIATORE
with roast potatoes & GF Yorkshire pud

If you're on a budget you can't always afford roast beef with Yorkshire puddings, so I've teamed my gluten-free Yorkshires with this tasty hunter's stew, or cacciatore as it's also called in Italy. The Yorkshire puds are perfect for dipping in the sauce at the end of the meal so this recipe has a few extra puds.

Serves 2 with extra Yorkshires

Ingredients for the chicken cacciatore:

1 tablespoon cooking oil
1 stalk of celery, finely diced
1 medium carrot, finely diced
1 medium onion. finely sliced
2 free-range chicken legs, skin on, plus the 2 wings for flavour
1 garlic clove, crushed
1 x 400g tin chopped tomatoes, plus ³/₄ the tin filled with water
Pinch of salt and pepper
Fresh rosemary sprigs
100ml red wine (optional)
10 pitted olives, halved (optional)

Ingredients for the roasties:

2 large peeled potatoes (Maris piper or king Edwards)
2 tablespoons olive oil
Pinch of salt

Ingredients for the Yorkshire pudding:

100g GF flour
3 eggs
150ml milk
Pinch of salt
Sunflower oil, for cooking

Serve with peas and carrots

Heat the oil in a high sided frying pan on a medium heat and add the chicken, turning for about 10 minutes, until golden. Add the chopped vegetables and garlic and keep cooking on a medium for 8-10 minutes, until soft, then add the salt and pepper.

Cook for 5 minutes then add the wine (if using) the chopped tomatoes, water and rosemary. Put on a lid and on a low heat simmer for about 25-30 minutes or until the chicken is cooked. Add a bit more water if it gets too dry.

While this is cooking, boil the peeled potatoes in salted water for 3-4 minutes, until just soft and then drain. Give them a little shake. Not too hard as you don't want them to break up, you just want them to fluff up around the edges.

While the potatoes are boiling, pour the olive oil in a roasting tin and put in a hot oven at 200°C. When the potatoes are ready, carefully take the roasting tin out of the oven, and tip the potatoes in. Turn each of the potatoes to coat them in the hot oil, and return the tray to the oven. If you're cooking parsnips add them here too.

Roast for 25-30 minutes until golden, turning only once or twice. The potatoes will need to be ready, taken out and kept warm when you cook the Yorkshire pudding, as you'll need the oven on high and you'll have to keep the door shut.

To make the Yorkshire pudding, whisk all the ingredients together except the oil and let stand. When you're ready turn up the oven to 220°C and heat a little oil in cups of the muffin tin. When hot, carefully pour the batter mixture in to each cup of the tin with a ladle and cook for 15-20 minutes, until golden. Don't open the door until cooked.

Top the cacciatore with a little chopped parsley and olives.

MEAL UNDER
£2.70
EACH

PIZZOCCHERI
with cabbage & potato

I've really wanted to recreate this dish since we went on holiday to the Italian Alps a few years ago. We found a hidden away restaurant in a little town I can't even remember the name of, but what I do remember is this dish. When I got home and looked up the recipe, and found out that buckwheat isn't a grain at all, it's a seed, I thought it would be perfect to use in one of my gluten-free budget recipe weeks.

Serves 2 with a bit of leftover pasta

Ingredients for the pizzoccheri pasta:
140g buckwheat flour, plus extra for dusting
½ teaspoon xanthan gum
1 small egg, lightly beaten
1 tablespoon milk
Warm water
Salt

Ingredients for the pasta sauce:
350g savoy cabbage, shredded
250g potatoes, chopped into chunks
70g butter
1 onion, thinly sliced
2 garlic cloves, thinly sliced
4 sage leaves, shredded
100g cheese, thinly sliced
Generous grinding of salt and pepper
1 tablespoon of olive oil

To make the gluten-free buckwheat pasta, Mix together the flour, xanthan gum and a pinch of salt into a mound in a bowl, or on your countertop if you're feeling Italian, and make a well in the centre.

Add the egg, 1 tablespoon of water, and the milk and gradually incorporate the flour with your fingers, adding more warm water if you need to. Knead until smooth.

Wrap in cling film and let rest at room temperature for about 30 minutes.

To make the pasta sauce, put the cabbage and potato with a pinch of salt into a pan with water. Bring to a boil, then lower the heat, and simmer for 20 minutes until the cabbage is tender and the potato is soft.

Cook the onion, garlic, and sage in the olive oil in a large saucepan, until soft and golden brown.

Now roll out the pasta dough on a lightly floured counter and cut into 2cm wide ribbons, about 12cm long. You won't need a machine for this one as it's supposed to be fairly thick pasta.

Add the pizzoccheri to the pan of cabbage and potato, and cook for about 5 minutes, then drain, and transfer the mixture to the larger onion pan and toss together.

Place a layer of pizzoccheri-vegetable mixture on the base of a serving dish, then a layer of broken cheese slices on top. Then continue with another layer of pasta and vegetables before finishing off with some broken cheese, a scatter of chopped sage and a grinding of black pepper. Serve hot.

MEAL UNDER £1 EACH

MEAL UNDER
£1.50
EACH

CORONATION CHICKEN
with curry rice

I remember when coronation chicken sandwiches were really popular, then it kind of went out of fashion as the original recipe is a bit of a faff. So this cheat's version is simple and quick to knock together. We sometimes even make it fresh for our packed lunches before work with leftover roast chicken, so it's perfect for a mid-week meal.

Serves 2 with leftover rice

Ingredients for the coronation chicken:
2 free-range chicken breasts, boiled and diced
4 tablespoons mayonnaise
4 teaspoons mango chutney
$1/2$ teaspoon curry powder
1 teaspoon garam masala
$1/2$ teaspoon turmeric
Salt, to taste
1 tablespoon flaked almonds (optional)
1 tablespoon sultanas (optional)
Handful of chopped coriander

Ingredients for the Curry rice:
1 medium onion, finely chopped
1-2 cloves of garlic crushed
1cm of finely chopped ginger
1 cup of rice
2 cups of water
1 teaspoon garam masala
1 teaspoon turmeric
1 teaspoon curry powder
1 tablespoon flaked almonds (optional)
1 tablespoon sultanas (optional)
Handful of chopped coriander
2 tablespoons olive oil
Salt, to taste

For the coronation chicken, firstly poach the chicken by putting the chicken breasts in a pan of cold water, then bringing it to a boil. Cover the saucepan and lightly simmer until the chicken breasts are cooked through, about 15-20 minutes. Remove the chicken from the saucepan and let it cool.

Mix the diced cooled chicken breast with the mayonnaise and mango chutney together with the curry spices. Season well and stir in some chopped coriander, flaked almonds and sultanas. Save back a little of the coronation chicken for a sandwich later in the week if you can.

To cook the curry rice firstly you need to boil the rice. The best way to cook rice that I've found is to measure a cup of rice in to a saucepan and rinse it a few times in clean water to wash off the starch. Afterwards drain the water and measure out 2 cups of water and add to the rice with a pinch of salt.

Bring the rice to the boil then let it simmer for about 10 minutes until all the water has soaked into the rice and disappeared. When you look into the pan the rice will have little dimples in the surface and it should be cooked perfectly. Take out a bit to test it. When ready pour into a sieve to completely drain any leftover water.

While the rice is cooking gently fry the onions in a tablespoon of oil, adding garlic and ginger after 5 minutes. Take out the softened onion mixture and with another tablespoon of oil fry the curry spices for a few minutes.

Pop the onions back into the frying pan and add the drained rice. Give it all a few minutes on a low heat to warm the rice through, stirring all the time. Season to taste, then add the chopped coriander, some flaked almonds and sultanas if you want and serve with the chicken.

GF BEEF LASAGNE
with salad

Just because you're gluten intolerant doesn't mean you have to miss out on family favourites, like this tasty lasagna. Sure you can pick up some expensive gluten-free pasta ready meals from the supermarket these days, but with this recipe being so easy to make, why would you want to?

Serves 2 with leftovers

Ingredients for the gluten free pasta:
300g gluten-free bread flour
2 teaspoons Xanthan gum
1 teaspoon salt
125ml water
1 tablespoon oil
2 eggs

Ingredients for the bolognese sauce:
1 tablespoon of oil
250g (1/2 packet) lean mince
2 garlic cloves, finely chopped
1 celery stalk, finely chopped
1 medium onion, finely chopped
2 tablespoons tomato purée
1/2 red pepper, finely chopped
200g (1/2 tin) tomatoes
100ml water
1 teaspoon dried oregano
Pinch of salt and pepper, to taste

Ingredients for the cheese sauce:
25g butter
25g gluten-free plain flour
400ml milk
100g Cheddar cheese
Pinch of salt and pepper, to taste

To make the fresh gluten-free pasta, make a well in the centre of your dry ingredients and add the wet ingredients.

Pull in the sides and mix together well then knead on a floured surface until it goes springy, about 5-10 minutes.

Add more flour or water if you need to. wrap it in cling film and pop it in the fridge for an hour. When you're ready to make the lasagna divide the pasta dough in 3 and roll out each one to about the size of your dish. A little wonky is fine.

Meanwhile, make the bolognese sauce, as the longer this rests the better it tastes. In a deep saucepan heat the oil and cook all the vegetables for about 10-15 minutes until soft, then add the mince beef and garlic and fry for about 5 minutes until browned.

Next add the tomatoes, water, purée and seasoning and bring to the boil. Then turn down to a simmer for at least 30 minutes, longer if you can. If it gets a bit dry add some more water. Stir every now and then to stop it sticking.

To make the cheese sauce, put a pan on a medium heat with the butter to melt. When the butter has melted, stir in the flour for a minute to make a paste, then turn down and gradually add the milk, whisking as you go, until lovely and smooth. Make sure you keep stirring so it doesn't burn on the bottom.

When the sauce has started to thicken add 75g of the Cheddar and season to taste.

Layer the lasagna finishing with the pasta, sheet and white sauce then the remaining cheese scattered on top. Bake at 180°C for 30 minutes until golden. Serve with some salad.

BEEF & BEAN ENCHILADAS
with tomato salsa

This recipe came about one day at the end of the week, when there wasn't much in the fridge except some leftover bolognese and some cheese. Making the mince go further, we added beans and wrapped it in homemade tortillas to create this delicious enchilada dish. For this version I've made gluten-free wraps as they're much cheaper and tastier than shop-bought ones.

Serves 2

Ingredients for the beef filling:
250g lean mince
$1/2$ medium onion, diced
$1/2$ red pepper, diced
1 celery, stalk diced
2 tablespoons tomato purée
200g ($1/2$ tin) tomatoes
100ml water
Salt and pepper, to taste
1 teaspoon ground cumin
$1/2$ teaspoon dried oregano
$1/2$ teaspoon chilli powder
1 garlic clove
400g tin red kidney beans

100g grated Cheddar cheese
Finely sliced chilli

Ingredients for the wraps:
250g gluten-free bread flour, plus extra for dusting
$1/2$ teaspoon xanthan gum
1 tablespoon oil
150ml water
$1/2$ teaspoon salt

Serve with tomato salsa, (see page 25)

To make the beef filling, in a deep saucepan heat the oil and fry all the vegetables for about 10-15 minutes until soft, then add the mince beef and garlic and fry for about 5 minutes until starting to brown.

Next add the tomatoes, water, purée and seasoning and bring to the boil. Turn down to a simmer for 15 minutes, then add the kidney beans and simmer for another 15 minutes, stirring every now and then to stop it sticking.

Next make the gluten-free wraps by making a well in the centre of your dry ingredients and pouring in the wet ingredients.

Pull in the sides and mix together well, then knead on a floured surface for about 5-10 minutes, until it goes springy.

Add more flour or water if you need to. Cover with a tea towel until you are ready to make the wraps. Divide the dough in 3 and roll out each one about the size of a tea plate.

Pile the beef filling in the middle of each wrap and fold over the ends then roll and place seam down in a small roasting tin, so they are snug. Repeat twice more and scatter over some grated cheese.

Bake in the oven at 190°C for about 20 minutes, or until the bread is cooked and the cheese is golden.

Serve with a scatter of chilli and some homemade salsa.

MEAL UNDER
£1.80
EACH

FRIED FISH IN GLUTEN FREE BATTER
With paprika chips & margarita salsa

Everyone enjoys traditional fish and chips, but if you can't have flour, getting a takeaway isn't an option. This recipe uses gluten-free flour mixed with fizzy spring water to help the batter to bubble just like the chippy one does – but unlike the local chip shop, I've added paprika and polenta to these chips to make them crunchy and included a zingy lime salsa dressing.

Serves 2

Ingredients for the fried fish in batter:
2 defrosted fish pieces
130g gluten-free flour, plus 3 tablespoons reserved in a bowl
180ml sparking water
$\frac{1}{2}$ teaspoon baking powder
Pinch of salt and pepper
Vegetable oil, for frying

Ingredients for the paprika chips:
2 large potatoes
1 teaspoon paprika
2 tablespoons dry polenta
$\frac{1}{2}$ teaspoon salt

Ingredients for the margarita salsa:
$\frac{1}{2}$ red onion, finely chopped
Handful of coriander, finely chopped
$\frac{1}{2}$ chilli, finely chopped
2 teaspoons lime juice
Splash of tequila (optional)
Pinch of salt and pepper

Lemon or lime wedges, to serve

Preheat the oven to 200°C.

In a deep bowl mix together the 130g of flour, salt, pepper and baking powder, then make a well in the middle and add the sparkling water. Whisk well until the batter is smooth. Let this rest while you get on with the other ingredients.

To make the chips, cut the potatoes into wedges and place them into a clean freezer bag with the paprika, polenta and salt. Give it all a good shake to evenly coat the potatoes.

Tip out the potato wedges onto a baking tray and drizzle over 1-2 tablespoons of oil. Roast in the oven for about 20-25 minutes, turning at least once, to stop them sticking.

To make the margarita salsa, mix all the ingredients together and season with more lime, salt or pepper until its taste is right for you.

Pat the fish dry and roll each fillet in the bowl of flour. This will help it dry out even more to stop it spitting when it goes in the hot oil.

Carefully heat up the oil in a large, deep saucepan so that a cube of bread should turn brown in one minute when dropped in.

Dip each of the fillets in the batter mixture until evenly covered and using tongs carefully lower into the hot oil. Deep-fry the fish for 4-6 minutes until golden brown and crisp, then drain on kitchen paper.

You can keep them warm in the oven while the chips finish cooking. Serve with the margarita salsa and lemon or lime wedges.

MEAL UNDER
£1.45
EACH

WEEK 8

①	2 loaves of sliced wholemeal bread	⑪	Fresh coriander
②	Olive spread	⑫	1.5kg plain flour
③	2 pints of soya milk	⑬	2 large aubergines
④	500g yellow or red split lentils	⑭	150g vegan Violife parmesan-style cheese
⑤	1kg onions	⑮	100g pine nuts
⑥	Bunch of spring onions	⑯	200g vegan Violife grated mozzarella-style cheese
⑦	Chillies	⑰	2.5kg potatoes
⑧	Ginger	⑱	186ml maple syrup
⑨	Garlic	⑲	200g cashews
⑩	420g cherry tomatoes	⑳	3 x 400g tin tomatoes

21 1 x 400g tin mixed beans	**31** 1 small cauliflower
22 1 x 400ml tin of coconut milk	**32** 1kg sweet potatoes
23 Radishes	**33** 1kg rice
24 2 little gem lettuces	**34** 2 lemons
25 1 cucumber	**35** 500g vegan Alpro natural yogurt
26 1 carrot	**36** 1kg red onions
27 500g macaroni	
28 500g vermicelli	
29 Packet of 3 peppers	
30 1kg frozen peas	Shopping list for lunch and dinner for 2 for 7 days

DAY-BY-DAY VEGAN
MENU FOR WEEK 8

Week 8 is vegan, which can be a bit of a challenge the first time you try it. I wasn't sure what was involved in a vegan diet when I first added one to my blog, but have since found and adjusted loads of great recipes that contain no dairy, eggs or honey. Specialist vegan food can be expensive, so any savings will help to keep to a tight budget, and if you already eat a vegan diet there will be certain ingredients like yeast flakes and maple syrup that you'll probably already use.

As a vegan diet needs non-meat protein I have added more nuts and pulses as well as plenty of vegetables and salad. The extra cost of vegan cheese means I've kept it to a minimum, really just for cheesy toppings. I think you're really going to enjoy this week of plant-based recipes.

Day 1
Lunch
Jacket potato

Dinner
Tarka dal with garlic naans & onion bhajis

Day 2
Lunch
Onion soup, (see page 34)

Dinner
Aubergine parmigiana

Day 3
Lunch
Leftover tarka dal and naan

Dinner
Aubergine katsu curry with rice and Japanese salad

Day 4
Lunch
Rice salad, (see page 21)

Dinner
Vegan mac & cheese

Day 5
Lunch
Sweet potato soup, (see page 35)

Dinner
Vegan vermicelli paella

Day 6
Lunch
Pasta salad

Dinner
Vegetable biryani

Day 7
Lunch
Leftover vegetable biryani with mint yogurt raita

Dinner
Gnocchi in tomato sauce with salad

TARKA DAL
with garlic Naans & onion bhajis

Dal is made all over the Indian subcontinent, and is a staple of most family meals. The name means dried split pulses, like lentils, peas and beans. If you've never had tarka dal before because you think its just some mashed up lentils, you're in for a treat with this recipe. It's full of flavour and with the homemade bhajis and naans makes for an every day Indian feast.

Serves 2 with leftovers

Ingredients for the tarka dal:

250g yellow dried split lentils, rinsed til the water runs clear
3 tablespoons vegetable oil
1 tablespoons cumin seeds
1 small onion, finely chopped
2 whole green chillies, pricked with a knife
2cm piece fresh ginger, peeled and cut into thin strips
3 garlic cloves, peeled and left whole
3 tomatoes
1 teaspoon ground turmeric
1 teaspoon garam masala
1 1/2 teaspoons ground coriander
salt and pepper, to taste
Handful of chopped fresh coriander leaves

Ingredients for the garlic Naans:

1 teaspoon of quick yeast
1 teaspoon of caster sugar
1/2 teaspoon of salt
300g strong flour, plus extra for rolling
1 tablespoon of olive oil
150ml natural yogurt
1 garlic clove, crushed
Sprig of coriander, chopped

Ingredients for the onion bhajis:

Vegetable oil, for frying
150g self-raising flour
1 teaspoon cumin seeds
1 teaspoon salt
1/2 teaspoon curry powder
1 teaspoon of ground coriander
1/4 teaspoon Baking powder
2 teaspoons garam masala
1 medium onion, thinly sliced
75ml cold water

Place the lentils and 900ml of water into a pan, stir well and bring to the boil. Skim off any froth that forms on the surface of the water with a spoon. Cover the pan with a lid and reduce the heat to a simmer. Stir regularly for 35-40 minutes, until the lentils are tender, adding more water if needed.

When the lentils have cooked, take them off the heat and whisk to break them down, then set aside to thicken and cool.

Meanwhile, heat the oil in a pan over a medium heat, and add the cumin seeds. Fry for 20-30 seconds until fragrant.

To this pan add the onion, chillies and ginger and fry for another 6-8 minutes until golden brown. Purée the garlic and tomatoes with a hand blender, then add to the pan and stir to combine.

Add the other ground spices and 100ml of water to the pan and stir well. Lightly season with salt and simmer over a medium heat for 15-20 minutes, or until the oil from the sauce has risen to the surface of the sauce.

Add the cooked lentils to the sauce and stir well, adding more water as necessary to loosen the mixture. Bring the mixture to the boil and season, to taste, with salt and pepper. Stir in the chopped coriander just before serving. You don't add salt until near the end as it can make the lentils hard. Serve with natural yogurt.

For the naan bread (see page 14)

For the onion bhajis, mix all the dry ingredients together in a large bowl, then add the sliced onion and stir. Next add the water and mix with your hands until everything is coated.

Heat 5cm of oil in a deep saucepan and gently fry a tablespoon of the mixture until golden on both sides, a few at a time. Pop them in a low oven to keep warm as you go.

MEAL UNDER
£1.80
EACH

AUBERGINE PARMIGIANA

Parmigiana is a Northern Italian dish similar to a Greek moussaka, but without the cinnamon and potato layers, This vegan version uses a white sauce mixture of blended cashews and yeast flakes to get that cheesy flavour, which even as a cheese eater I really enjoyed. We'll definitely be making this parmigiana again.

Serves 2 plus leftovers

Ingredients for the tomato sauce:

2 garlic cloves, crushed
3/4 of an onion, chopped
1 teaspoon mixed herbs
400g tin chopped tomatoes
2 tablespoons tomato purée
1 glass red wine or 2 tablespoons red wine vinegar
1 tablespoon sugar
Salt and pepper, to taste

Ingredients for the aubergine parmigiana:

1 large aubergine, cut into 5mm slices
1 tablespoon olive oil, plus extra for brushing
30g vegan parmesan-style cheese
85g white bread crumbs
30g pine nuts (optional)
100g vegan mozzarella cheese, torn into small chunks

Ingredients for the vegan white sauce:

2 tablespoons yeast flakes
1/4 onion
90g cashews
Pinch of salt
250ml water
Blended until totally smooth, no grainy bits

To make the tomato sauce, heat the oil in a large saucepan, then add the onion, garlic and mixed herbs and cook gently for a few minutes. Pour in the tomatoes, wine or vinegar, purée and sugar, then gently simmer for 20-25 minutes until thickened a little. Taste it and season with salt and pepper and more purée if needed.

Next blend the white sauce ingredients together until totally smooth with no grainy bits, then pour into a small saucepan and gently heat for about 10 minutes, until thickened.

Meanwhile, heat a griddle or frying pan on medium, then brush the aubergine slices on both sides with olive oil.

Griddle in batches. You want each slice softened and slightly charred. Don't have the heat too high, or they'll char before softening.

In another bowl mix 25g of the grated parmesan with the bread crumbs and pine nuts, and put to one side.

Preheat the oven to 220°C.

In a large pie dish, spread a thin layer of the tomato sauce over the base. Next a layer of aubergine slices, then the white sauce and finally the bread crumb mixture.

Repeat the layers, then finish with the last of the white sauce. Scatter over the mozzarella.

Bake for about 20-25 minutes, then grill until the cheesy topping is crisp and golden.

Serve with a small side salad if you like.

AUBERGINE KATSU CURRY
with rice and Japanese salad

Katsu curry is really popular at the moment, but if you don't eat meat it doesn't mean you can't enjoy this version with aubergines, or eggplants as our American friends say. It's really easy to make the katsu sauce and breaded aubergines using leftover crusts, but there's also a delicious Japanese salad dressing recipe too. I have provided an easy-to-follow cooking video on my FoodologistGirl YouTube channel.

Serves 2

Ingredients for the aubergine katsu curry:
1 large aubergine, sliced
4 tablespoons flour
2-3 slices of bread, made into fine bread crumbs
4-5 tablespoons vegetable oil
Pinch of salt and pepper

Ingredients for the katsu sauce:
1 medium onion, finely chopped
1 tablespoon vegetable oil
4 garlic cloves, crushed
2 cm fresh ginger
3 tablespoons medium curry powder
1 tablespoon maple syrup
1 tablespoon garam masala
1 tablespoon flour
Pinch of salt and pepper
1 tin coconut milk.

Ingredients for the rice:
1 cup basmati rice to 2 cups of water, plus a pinch salt

Ingredients for the Japanese salad dressing:
2 tablespoons of rice or white wine vinegar
2 tablespoons soy sauce
2 teaspoons caster sugar
1/2 small onion, finely chopped
2 cm fresh ginger, chopped
2 teaspoons tomato purée
2 tablespoons vegetable oil
Pinch of salt and pepper, to taste

Ingredients for the Japanese salad:
Cucumber, radishes, carrot peppers, lettuce as photo

Mix the flour with enough water to make a paste and water and cover the sliced aubergine, then cover in fine bread crumbs.

Shallow fry til golden, then bake in the oven for 20-25 minutes.

Next, make the katsu curry sauce by gently frying the finely chopped onion, and garlic until soft. Then add curry powder, garam masala, and the flour with a little salt and pepper. After a few minutes add the maple syrup.

Cook this for a couple more minutes before adding the coconut milk. Hand whisk if it looks a little lumpy. Simmer for about 20 minutes until it reduces down and thickens. It should go a darker coffee colour.

Meanwhile cook the rice as page 21 Brush a little oil on the inside of a small bowl, fill with cooked sticky rice and press down.

To make the salad dressing, put all the ingredients in a clean jam jar. Do up the lid and give it a good shake. This will last for a couple of weeks in the fridge for other salads.

To make the salad use ingredients like radishes, finely sliced carrot, peppers, green beans, cucumber, spring onions etc.

To serve, tip out the rice, then lay out the aubergine and pour on the katsu sauce. Arrange the salad and drizzle with the dressing.

Cook extra rice to make a rice salad for another day.

VEGAN MAC & CHEESE

Macaroni cheese is a quick and easy meal to throw together for most of us, but if you're eating a plant-based diet it's a bit more difficult and expensive using cheese and milk substitutes. This recipe uses blended cashews which are a great source of protein, but also means you use a lot less of that expensive vegan cheese.

Serves 2

Ingredients for mac & cheese:
150g macaroni
70g vegan mozzarella cheese
A few spring onion tops, sliced

Ingredients for the white sauce:
2 tablespoons yeast flakes
2 spring onions
90g cashews
$1/2$ teaspoon salt
300ml water

1 teaspoon Dijon mustard
30g vegan parmesan-style cheese

Preheat the oven to 200°C.

Firstly cook the macaroni according to the packet instructions.

Next blend the white sauce ingredients together until totally smooth with no grainy bits, then pour in to a small saucepan and gently heat for about 10 minutes, until it thickens.

Stir in the mustard and vegan parmesan cheese until melted, then add the drained macaroni.

Stir well , then pour into 1 or 2 ovenproof dishes.

Scatter over the mozzarella and bake for 20-25 minutes until golden and bubbling.

Scatter over the spring onion tops and serve with a small salad.

Cook extra macaroni to make pasta salad for lunches.

MEAL UNDER
£1.30
EACH

Vegan vermicelli
PAELLA

Paella comes in many forms, depending on where in Spain you're making it. Instead of the risotto rice I would normally use, I saw that some paella chefs use vermicelli, so for this vegan version I decided to use all the flavours of a tradional paella without the meat and fish and using these fine noodles instead. Is it still a paella? I'm $^1/_{16}$ Spanish, and I say it is.

Serves 2

Ingredients for the vermicelli paella:
150g broken vermicelli
$^1/_2$ red pepper, diced
$^1/_2$ green pepper, diced
1 tablespoon olive oil
1 medium onion, sliced
3 garlic cloves, crushed
70g frozen peas
400g tin chopped tomatoes
1 teaspoon paprika
Pinch of salt

Added options ingredients:
You could add green beans, artichoke hearts or mushrooms - whatever you like

Preheat the oven to 200°C.

In a large frying pan, break and spread the noodles to form a single layer. Toast for about 10 minutes, until golden brown. Watch them carefully, so they don't burn, then set aside.

Clean the frying pan and gently cook the onions in the olive oil, for about 10 minutes.

Add crushed garlic and cook on a medium heat, for about 3 minutes. Add the peppers, paprika and salt and cook for another 10 minutes.

Add the tin of tomatoes, then half-fill the empty tin with water and add. Bring to the boil, then add the frozen peas and keep cooking at a simmer. Scatter the noodles all over the pan and carefully mix until well combined with all the ingredients.

Let it simmer for about 15 minutes, until the noodles are tender. Add a touch more water if it's getting to dry. Taste to see if it needs more salt or paprika.

Remove from heat and pour into an ovenproof dish, then pop it in the oven for 8-10 minutes, until most of the liquid has been absorbed and the noodles start to brown slightly.

Serve with a squeeze of lemon and a scatter of chopped parsley.

VEGETABLE BIRYANI
with mint yogurt raita

This is a new recipe for our family, but now a firm favourite. We often made biryani with leftover curry, but this simple recipe uses fresh vegetables in one roasting pan and couldn't be easier. With cauliflower, sweet potato, onion and peas you're even getting 4 of your 5-a-day with this tasty meal.

Serves 2 with leftovers

Ingredients for the curry paste:
2 onions
2 garlic cloves
1 teaspoon ground ginger
1 teaspoon paprika
2 teaspoons garam masala
1 teaspoon turmeric
$1/2$ teaspoon salt
2 tablespoons cooking oil
1 tablespoon tomato purée
$1/2$ teaspoon chilli flakes
Spices for toasting: 3 teaspoons cumin seeds
2 teaspoons coriander seeds
1 teaspoon black peppercorns

Ingredients for the vegetable biryani:
1 tablespoon vegetable oil
1 small cauliflower, broken into small florets
1 medium sweet potato, peeled and cubed
1 onion, sliced
$1/2$ litre hot vegetable stock
2 tablespoons medium curry paste (see above)
1 red chilli, de-seeded and finely chopped
Pinch of turmeric
1 teaspoon mustard seed (black or white)
250g basmati rice
70g frozen peas
1 lemon, juice only
Handful of cashews or peanuts

Ingredients for the cheat's mint raita:
1 teaspoon mint sauce
3 tablespoons vegan natural yogurt
2 inch piece of cucumber, grated

If you're feeling lazy you can buy a jar of curry paste, or alternatively you can make your own by toasting the spices in a dry pan, shaking them until they are going golden and start to smell delicious. Crush these until powdered.

Then peel the garlic and ginger and add all the rest of the ingredients, including the toasted spices, in a blender and whizz together. This is your curry paste.

Preheat the oven to 220°C.

Pour the oil into a large roasting tin and put in the oven for a couple of minutes to heat through.

Add all the vegetables, except the peas, to the tin, stirring to coat them in the hot oil. Season with salt and pepper and bake for about 15 minutes until just beginning to brown.

While the vegetables are roasting, stir together the stock, curry paste, chilli, turmeric and mustard seeds.

Scatter the rice and frozen peas with the cooked vegetables in the tin, then pour over the stock mixture.

Lower the oven to 190°C. Then cover the dish tightly with foil and bake in the oven for about 30 minutes, until the rice is tender and the liquid has been absorbed.

Stir in a squeeze of lemon juice and season with a little salt, then scatter over the coriander and nuts. Serve with a bowl of plain yogurt or raita.

To make the cheat's raita cut the cucumber in half and scoop out and discard the seeds. Grate the cucumber, pat the excess water off with a paper towel and mix into the yogurt with the mint sauce. Season to taste.

MEAL UNDER
75p
EACH

GNOCCHI IN TOMATO SAUCE
with salad

The first time I made gnocchi was a few years ago, and it was a disaster. My potatoes were too wet and then as I tried to cook the gnocchi in the water as I would pasta, it all just disintegrated and all I ended up with was cloudy water. I now know not to boil but gently poach your gnocchi and that you need to use totally dry potatoes mixed with the flour.

Serves 2

Ingredients for the gnocchi:
250g potatoes made in to mash
120g plain flour
2 tablespoons dried oregano
1 teaspoon salt

Ingredients for the tomato sauce:
1 tablespoon olive oil
1 onion, chopped
1 red pepper, de-seeded and finely chopped
2 garlic cloves, finely chopped
400g tin chopped tomatoes
1 tablespoon balsamic vinegar
1 tablespoon tomato purée
30g vegan mozzarella cheese, torn into small chunks
Handful of basil leaves, torn (optional)

Firstly make your gnocchi by either using leftover mashed potatoes, or boiling a few potatoes and draining them, then letting them cool and making some mash.

Next add the flour gradually and work it into the potato, add the salt and oregano, and more flour, then knead until all the flour is used up and you have a dough that isn't sticky but soft.

Divide the dough into 4 and roll out into a thin sausage shape about 1cm thick. Cut this into 2cm pieces, then roll each one up the back of a fork to create a slight indent. This will help hold onto the sauce when you're eating it.

Leave these separated on a floured board while you get the tomato sauce ready.

For the tomato sauce, heat the oil in a large frying pan, then soften the onion and pepper for about 5 minutes.

Stir in the garlic and fry for 1 minute more, then tip in the tomatoes and bring to the boil, then to a simmer.

Add the gnocchi, and gently stir once.

Simmer for 10-15 minutes, stirring occasionally, until the gnocchi is soft and the sauce has thickened. Season with salt and pepper, then transfer to a large ovenproof dish.

Scatter with the vegan mozzarella, then grill for 5-6 minutes until the cheese is bubbling and golden.

Scatter with a little basil if you're using it, and serve with a small fresh salad.

Vegan
CHOCOLATE CAKE

Just because you follow a plant-based diet doesn't mean you can't have indulgent chocolate cake. This one has a secret ingredient of avocado to make the frosting really creamy. Everyone that tried this delicious cake couldn't even tell, but they all enjoyed it.

Cuts into 12 slices

Ingredients for the cake:
500ml unsweetened soya or almond milk
150ml vegetable oil
2 teaspoons vanilla extract
325g plain flour
400g sugar
75g cocoa powder
1 teaspoon salt
1 teaspoon cider vinegar
2 teaspoons bicarbonate of soda

Ingredients for the frosting:
60ml vegetable oil
60ml water
$1/2$ tablespoon vanilla extract
150g ripe avocado, cubed
30g cocoa powder
100g icing sugar
Pinch of salt

Preheat the oven to 180°C and line two 8 inch cake tins with greaseproof paper.

Mix together all of the cake ingredients, except the vinegar and bicarbonate of soda. Once the batter is smooth, add them on opposite sides of the bowl to ensure they don't react prematurely.

Now blend for long enough to mix into the batter. But don't over mix or the cake won't rise.

Divide the batter between the tins and bake in the oven for about 55-60 minutes. Test with a skewer to check they're cooked about 15 minutes before the end. Cover with foil half way through so they don't burn.

Leave the cakes to stand for 10 minutes before removing from their tins and cool on a wire rack.

Cut the domed top off one of the cakes to make it flat.

Blend all the frosting ingredients together with a whisk until smooth and creamy.

Spread a thick layer of frosting on top of the flattened cake, then put the second cake on top and spread the remaining frosting over the cake.

Eat on the day or it can keep in a sealed container in the refrigerator for a few days.

Retro

QUEEN OF PUDDINGS

This dessert is an old fashioned, traditional, money saving recipe that uses up leftover bread crumbs to make the sponge. With the piped meringue it looks quite posh and fit for a queen even though it only costs pennies to make. Under the meringue you can use any jam, fruit preserve, lemon curd or even some homemade marmalade, whatever you have knocking about.

Serves 2-4

Ingredients for the base:
600ml milk
25g butter, plus extra for greasing the dish
Zest of 1 lemon
50g sugar
3 egg yolks
75g bread crumbs

Ingredients for the meringue:
125g caster sugar
3 eggs whites
3-4 tablespoons of raspberry jam

Preheat the oven to 170°C and grease a deep 1.4 litre ovenproof dish with butter.

First, gently warm the milk in a saucepan. Add the butter, lemon zest and sugar, then stir until dissolved.

Whisk the egg yolks in a bowl, then pour the warm milk into the eggs, and keep whisking.

Scatter the bread crumbs in the base of the dish and pour over the milky custard, then leave to stand for about 15-20 minutes to let the bread crumbs absorb all of the liquid.

Transfer the dish to a large high-sided roasting tin and fill the tin halfway with hot water to make a waterbath. Bake the custard mixture in the preheated oven for about 25-30 minutes until it has set slightly. Then remove from the oven and set aside to cool.

After it has cooled, spread the raspberry jam over the top then make the meringue topping.

In a clean, dry bowl whisk the egg whites, using an electric whisk, until stiff peaks form. Add the sugar a little at a time while still whisking. Transfer the meringue mixture to a piping bag and cover the top like the photo. Alternatively just dollop spoonfuls until the base is covered.

Set the oven temperature to 150°C and put the pudding in the oven without the waterbath for about 25-30 minutes until the meringue is golden all over.

Serve while still warm, but I found it microwaved well as leftovers too.

Yogurt cake
CROWN

I'm not sure where yogurt cake originated from – Italy, France or Germany – but whoever came up with this delicious, simple to make recipe deserves a medal. Just look at how short the instructions are. Although you can add fruit or chocolate to the sponge, I've given you a simple lemon and vanilla recipe to start you off.

Cuts into 8-10 slices

Ingredients for the cake:
150g plain yogurt
150ml vegetable oil
3 eggs, separated into whites and yolks
250g caster sugar
1 teaspoon vanilla extract
Zest of 1 lemon
250g plain flour or gluten free flour
1 teaspoon icing sugar, for dusting

Preheat the oven to 180°C.

Grease and lightly flour a bundt ring cake tin.

Whisk the egg whites until firm and set to one side.

Next whisk the yogurt with the egg yolks and sugar, then add the oil, whisking as you do. Next add the lemon zest and the vanilla extract.

Now add the flour, still mixing it all together.

Lastly fold in the egg whites until completely mixed.

Pour in to the tin and bake for 30-35 minutes.

Test with a skewer, and if ready take it out and let stand in its tin for about 10 minutes before turning out onto a cooling rack.

Before serving, dust over a little icing sugar.

CREAMY RICE PUDDING
with orange and sultana topping

I know rice pudding sounds like boring school dinners, but you haven't tried this rice pudding. Made with double cream it's a million miles away from those school days, and with the orange zest and sultana topping it gets a gold star from me.

Serves 2

Ingredients for the rice pudding:
100g pudding rice
$\frac{1}{2}$ litre milk
40g caster sugar
1 teaspoon vanilla extract
Good pinch of grated nutmeg
Handful of sultanas
100g double cream

Ingredients for the topping:
25g sultanas
Zest and juice of 1 orange

Added options ingredients:
You can use lots of different toppings like fresh fruit, Jam or just a teaspoon of brown sugar

To make the pudding, bring the milk to the boil with the sugar, vanilla and nutmeg.

Add the rice, stir well and simmer gently, stirring every now and then for 30 minutes, or until the rice is softened. Don't let it catch on the bottom and burn.

Remove from the heat, and leave to cool, then stir in the cream and put in the fridge until ready to serve.

For the orange and sultana topping, in a microwavable bowl mix half the zest and all the juice of the orange with the sultanas and microwave for 1 minute.

Let them stand for another minute so that the sultanas soften by soaking up the juice. Spoon on top of the rice pudding and scatter some zest for decoration.

APPLE & APRICOT PASTRY PUFFS

Makes 2

Ingredients for the pastry puffs:
100g puff pastry
1 apple, thinly sliced
2 tablespoons apricot jam
Egg or milk, to wash
1 teaspoon caster sugar
Dusting of icing sugar

Using the leftover pastry, roll out and cut it into 2 squares or rectangles about 4-6 inches long. The exact size isn't too important, it just needs to be big enough to hold the apple.

Core and slice the apple thinly and pop into a bowl of water with a squeeze of lemon to stop the slices going brown.

In the middle of each pastry square place a dollop of apricot jam. Then lay out the apple slices slightly on top of each other as per the photo.

Using either egg or milk brush over the pastry to help it turn golden. Then sprinkle over a small amount of sugar.

Bake in the oven for about 15 minutes until the pastry has puffed up and turned golden. Dust with icing sugar just before serving hot or cold with cream or custard.

MERINGUE FRUIT NESTS

Makes 4

Ingredients for the meringues:
3 medium egg whites
100g caster sugar
Pinch of salt

Ingredients for the fruit:
100g frozen fruit
1 tablespoon sugar
1 tablespoon water

Ingredients for the whipped cream:
150ml double cream
1 tablespoon icing sugar

Preheat the oven to 150°C

Put the egg whites into a large, clean bowl and beat with a handheld electric whisk until they hold stiff peaks. Gradually add the sugar and pinch of salt, whisking constantly, until the mixture becomes thick and glossy.

Spoon or pipe the meringue into nest shapes on greaseproof paper on a baking tray, then bake for about 1 hour or until the meringue is golden.

While the meringues are cooking, prepare the fruit by heating it in a saucepan with the water and sugar for about 10 minutes until it starts to get soft and squishy. Let it cool.

When the meringues are cooled, whip some double cream with the icing sugar. Fill the nests with the cream and the cooked fruit. Serve straight away.

Gluten-free
PINEAPPLE UPSIDE DOWN CAKES

This recipe is an old school favourite, I even remember making it in one of my few cookery classes as a teen. I've made this version gluten free, but it's still light and fluffy which is delicious with a creamy topping. I used the leftover pineapple slices from some of the other recipes in this book so it's a win, win here.

Makes 4

Ingredients for the topping:
4 pineapple rings
4 glacé cherries
1 tablespoon golden or white caster sugar
20g butter

Ingredients for the sponge:
160g plain gluten-free flour
$1/4$ teaspoon Xanthan gum
1 teaspoon GF baking powder
$1/2$ teaspoon ground cinnamon
$1/4$ teaspoon salt
200g caster sugar
110g butter
2 eggs
$1/2$ teaspoon vanilla essence
40ml milk

Preheat the oven to 180°C.

Firstly cream together the butter and sugar for the topping. Place a pineapple ring in the bottom of 4 small ovenproof bowls and pop a cherry in the middle of each one, then scatter the sugar cream over them.

Next cream together the rest of the sugar with the butter, then whisk in the eggs, vanilla essence and milk.

In another bowl stir together the flour, Xanthan gum, salt, cinnamon and baking powder.

Pour this into the eggy mixture and mix together well. Fill the ovenproof bowls, leaving an inch at the top and bake in the oven for about 20 minutes.

Check with a clean skewer after 15 minutes as the size and shape of the bowl will make a difference to the timing.

Serve with cream or custard.

LEMON CHEESECAKES
Gluten-free and vegetarian

I've made a few cheesecakes over the years, and I love this one with the fruit jelly top, so I had to add it to this book. This time I've made the base with gluten-free biscuits and instead of using my normal gelatine leaves for the jelly, I tried out the Vege-Gel sachets. They took a bit of practice and the first couple didn't set well. But this recipe version worked fine – it's just lucky my family like cheesecake!

Cuts into 8 slices

Ingredients for the base:
160g pack digestive biscuits
100g butter, melted
½ tablespoon maple syrup

Ingredients for the lemon filling:
200g cream cheese
250g ricotta
100g caster sugar
Zest and juice of 1 large lemon

Ingredients for the lemonade jelly layer:
1 sachet of Vege-Gel
2 pared, wide strips of lemon skin
Juice of 1 lemon
100g caster sugar
250ml sugar-free lemonade

Firstly put the biscuits in a food processor and whizz into fine crumbs, then pour in the melted butter and syrup and mix. If you don't have a food processor you can do this by breaking up the biscuits in a freezer bag with a rolling pin.

Pour the crumb mixture into a loose bottom cake tin and pat down until firm. Put in the fridge to harden for at least 30 minutes.

Whisk the cream cheese, ricotta and sugar in a mixing bowl until smooth. Add the lemon zest and juice.

Spread on top of the chilled biscuit base and level with a spatula. Chill for a least 2 hours until it has set.

To make the lemonade for the jelly layer, in a pan put the pared lemon zests, sugar and juice. Warm gently to dissolve the sugar.

Meanwhile mix the Vege-Gel in a jug with half the lemonade.

Remove the lemon skin from the pan, then mix in the Vege-Gel.

Turn the heat up to just about boiling, then turn off.

Mix in the remaining lemonade to help it cool quicker, then allow to cool a little more before carefully pouring it over the chilled cheesecake layer.

Keep checking it hasn't started setting before you pour but it must be a bit cooler before touching the cream cheese.

Leave it to set in the fridge for a couple of hours.

Traditional
MANCHESTER FLAN

This Manchester flan dish is a variation of the earlier Victorian era Manchester pudding dish written about by the famous cookery writer, Mrs Beeton. The simple shortcrust pastry dish is great for using up leftover ingredients from other recipes in this book, including the desiccated coconut and egg yolks.

Cuts in to 8-10 slices

Ingredients for the pastry:
300g plain flour
150g cold butter, cubed
25g icing sugar
4-5 tablespoons water

Ingredients for the custard filling:
450ml whole milk
3 large egg yolks
60g caster sugar
30g plain flour
2 teaspoons vanilla extract

4-5 tablespoons raspberry jam
80g desiccated coconut, toasted
A few glacé cherries

To make the shortcrust pastry, put the flour and icing sugar in a large bowl and add the cold cubes of butter.

Use your fingertips to rub the butter into the flour until you have a mixture that resembles coarse bread crumbs with no large lumps of butter remaining. Try to keep the butter as cold as you can as this will make nicer pastry.

Using a fork, stir in just enough of the cold water to bind the dough together in to a ball. Wrap the dough in clingfilm and chill in the fridge for about 10-15 minutes before using.

After the pastry has chilled, heat the oven to 190°C.

Roll out the pastry, then lay it with overhang for shrinkage in a 25cm loose bottom flan tin and blind bake it by putting some greaseproof paper on top and filling it with dried or ceramic beans. Cook for 18-20 minutes, then take out the beans, cut the pastry edges flush and cook for another 10 minutes.

Take out and let cool a little before spreading the jam over the bottom of the pastry and scattering over half the coconut.

To make the custard, heat the milk in a saucepan to just below boiling.

In a bowl mix in the egg yolks, sugar and vanilla extract together with the flour until smooth, then pour in the hot milk, keep stirring.

Now rinse out the pan and pour this mixture back in. Then bring to the boil, stirring for about 2-3 minutes, until thickened.

Allow to cool slightly before pouring into the pastry case and sprinkling with the rest of the coconut. Add the cherries and chill for about 4 hours until set. Then cut into slices.

FRUIT COBBLER

The best thing about frozen fruit, apart from it being cheap, is that you only need to use enough for your recipe and the rest pops back in the freezer for another day. No waste. We often forage for wild fruit in the autumn, even in urban areas, There's loads of blackberry bushes if you know where to look. You could make a winter crumble with them, or for a change this delicious fruit cobbler.

Serves 2-4

Ingredients for the fruit filling:
450g frozen fruit (winter mix)
2 tablespoons sugar
Splash of water

Ingredients for the cobbler pastry:
180g self-raising flour
45g butter
6-7 tablespoons milk

Ingredients for the cobbler sugar:
2 tablespoons brown sugar, plus another teaspoon
40g soft butter
1/2 teaspoon cinnamon (optional)

Firstly stew your fruit by putting it in a saucepan with the sugar and water on a medium heat for about 10 minutes, until the fruit softens.

Pour in to a small oven proof dish.

Next make the pastry by using your fingertips to rub the butter into the flour until you have a mixture that resembles bread crumbs. Then using a fork, stir in just enough of the milk to bind the dough together into a ball.

Roll out the pastry to about 4mm and spread over the softened butter. Next sprinkle over 2 tablespoons of the brown sugar and cinnamon if using..

Slice the pasty into 2 cm strips and roll into wheels.

Place each wheel over the stewed fruit.

Sprinkle over the teaspoon of brown sugar and bake in the oven for about 20 minutes until the pastry is golden and cooked.

Serve warm with cream, Ice cream or custard.

SUMMER PUDDING

Cuts into 6 slices

750g frozen mixed summer fruit
185g caster sugar
$1/4$ medium loaf of white bread, slightly stale
(Cut off the crusts but save these for making
into bread crumbs for other recipes)

Place the fruit and sugar in a pan and gently bring to the boil.

While the fruit is simmering, cut a large circle out of one slice of bread to fit in the bottom of a bowl, then cut the remaining slices into triangular wedges. Dip one side of the bread circle into the juices in the pan and place in the bottom of the pudding basin, juice side down.

Next do the same with the bread triangles, and place them around the edge of the bowl, with the dipped side facing outwards. When the bowl is completely lined, spoon all of the fruit and its juices into the pudding basin. Trim the tips of bread from around the edge and cover the top of the fruit with more bread.

Use a saucer that fits inside the bowl. Place it on top then weigh it down with tins of baked beans, and place in the fridge overnight. Turn the pudding out, cut into thick slices.

VEGAN CHOCOLATE BROWNIES

Cuts into 9 slices

5 tablespoons sunflower oil
200g dairy-free dark chocolate
180g self-raising flour
3 heaped teaspoons cocoa powder
180g caster sugar
230ml soya milk
Pinch of salt
1 teaspoon vanilla extract
2 tablespoons peanut butter (crunchy or smooth)

Preheat the oven to 180°C, and line a 20cm square baking tin, with greaseproof paper.

Melt 150g of the chocolate in a heatproof bowl over a saucepan of boiling water.

While the chocolate is melting, mix the flour, cocoa powder, sugar and a pinch of salt in a large bowl.

Next add in the vanilla extract, oil, soya milk and melted chocolate and stir until combined.

Stir in the remaining broken chocolate and the peanut butter.

Pour the mixture in the tin and spread out. Bake in the oven for 22-25 minutes, until cooked on the outside, but still gooey in the middle. Leave to cool slightly before turning out on a cooling rack and slice in to squares.

TIRAMISU

A few years ago now, when I was first learning to cook, I did a few evening classes of Italian cookery. One of the recipes we were taught by our lovely Italian teacher was this classic favourite, tiramisu. I've adapted this recipe slightly to make it cheaper by using ricotta instead of mascarpone, and dropping the liqueur, but it's still just as tasty, and I'm sure she wouldn't mind.

Serves 2

Ingredients for the tiramisu:
100g (½ packet) sponge finger biscuits
2 small eggs
1 mug strong black coffee, cooled
4 tablespoons sugar
125g (½ packet) ricotta cheese
Dusting of cocoa powder

Added options ingredients:
1 tablespoon Tia Maria or Marsala can be added to the coffee mixture

Firstly separate the egg yolks into one bowl, and whites in another.

Whisk the whites until firm.

Add 2 tablespoons of sugar to the cold black coffee and the liqueur if using, and stir well.

Whisk the egg yolks with 2 tablespoons of sugar, then add the ricotta and whisk that in.

Now carefully fold in the egg whites into the ricotta mixture. Try to keep as much air in as you can.

Next dip the sponge biscuits into the sweetened coffee. Be quick though, as they'll fall apart if you're too slow.

Put a layer of the sponge into the bottom of the glass, then a generous helping of the cream mixture.

Repeat the sponge and cream layers, then dust over the cocoa powder.

Crumble over a dry sponge biscuit just before serving.

This can be made a few hours beforehand and kept in the fridge, or made there and then in about 10 minutes, if you already have cold coffee.

INDEX

Jane Ashley is a graphic designer who lives with her husband and daughter in London. She was inspired to try feeding her family on an extraordinarily tight budget after volunteer cooking for a night shelter and having to produce nutritious, low-cost meals. Her first book *Home Economics, How to eat like a king,* published by Short Books, came out in 2018 and was designed for families of four.

You can find her blog *EatNotSpend* for other money saving recipes. Plus cooking videos can also be found on the FoodologistGirl YouTube channel.

I'd like to thank my husband Phil who again took all the photos for this book, plus makes the funny cooking videos for me. You're so talented and are happy to help with my mad ideas.

Also eagle-eyed Luna for correcting my appalling grammar, spelling and mistakes.

To Emily and Ruth for again being my guinea pigs and letting me feed them with new recipes.

To everyone that visits my blog, listens to me rant on Twitter, watches me show off on Instagram and visit my Facebook, thank you for supporting me.